Humbug To Happiness

Humbug To Happiness

Breaking The Chains of the Past

David A. Gibbs M.A. LMHC, CAP, ICADC

Foreword by
Abbey Danneman

Illustrated by
David A. Gibbs

Humbug to Happiness
© 2016 David A. Gibbs M.A. LMHC, CAP, ICADC
All rights reserved.

Publisher: David Gibbs
Florida

ISBN-13: 9781518634949
ISBN-10: 151863494X
Library of Congress Control Number: 2015919653
CreateSpace Independent Publishing Platform
North Charleston, South Carolina

Dedication

Ultimately, there are a number of forces that this book is dedicated to. First and foremost is my higher power. It is my hope that my words and deeds please the energy that continues to guide my purpose. Second, I would like to dedicate this book to all the individuals my higher power has seen fit for me to serve—the men and women who have played a significant part in the journey of this book by telling their stories. Specifically, it is dedicated to the knowledge of their true purpose and the miracle that is their master design. Moreover, this book is dedicated to the inner children of these men and women, who have now been set free from the imprisonment of the humbug messages that plagued them. Today they can participate in the celebration of their renewal in recognizing the gift of their true purpose in this life. Last but not least, this book is dedicated to my parents. I thank them for all their love and support through the good, the bad, and the ugly.

A man's mind may be likened to a garden, which may be intelligently cultivated or allowed to run wild; but whether cultivated or neglected, it must, and will, bring forth.

—James Allen, *As a Man Thinketh*

Contents

Foreword

It's a real honor to be sitting here today, writing the foreword to David Gibbs's book, *Humbug to Happiness*. David and I have been coworkers for many years, but we're great friends as well. We share a great deal of love, respect, and, more than anything else, pure laughter.

As you'll soon discover, David is an amazing writer, but he's far more than that. He is a dedicated professional and friend to many. He is one of the most talented, caring, passionate men I know, and he is gifted in so many areas of his life. David is a believer—spiritually beautiful and most obviously dedicated to all the special individuals he works with. He shares his gifts through his amazing smile.

For many years, David has been working on creating a book that identifies with all types of people who strive to make changes in their lives. Now it's finally here! *Humbug to Happiness* is a book for everyone, regardless of age, socioeconomic status, religion, race, or gender. I know and believe you are going to love this book. It's filled with wisdom and great examples about struggles people go through in life. David is able to get right to the heart of the matter in an honest, respectful, and lighthearted way.

My greatest hope is that all people will learn to live happier, more peaceful lives and will enjoy *Humbug to Happiness*!

Florida, 2013   Abbey Danneman

Introduction

Who I am is of little consequence. However, the message I have to offer is one deserving of your remembrance. The message I bring to you is one of *hope*—the *hope* of finding *home*.

Home is a place we all must find, child. It's not just a place where you eat or sleep. Home is knowing. Knowing your mind, knowing your heart, knowing your courage.

If we know ourselves, we're always home, anywhere.

—*The Wizard of Oz*

My friend, welcome home! I know your struggle in making the decision to seek help for yourself or a loved one is heavy. I ask that you allow yourself the opportunity to journey with me through *Humbug to Happiness*.

I'm here to ease your burden as you journey down this confusing and often frustrating path. Allow me to partner with you in developing an understanding that there is much you have to offer in this journey called your life. The humbug messages of your past have corrupted this understanding for you or your loved one. However, today there is a way to reclaim what you have been robbed of by your humbug messages!

Humbug to Happiness offers a dynamic and unique philosophy. I have worked tirelessly to find this philosophy to gain clarity throughout the twenty-plus years of my career. In the end, it is imperative that we all understand that there are no strangers among us.

What is it, you ask, that I have found? I have found *home*, here within the pages of *Humbug to Happiness*. During our journey, we will work as a family dedicated to helping those who enter this journey by enveloping them with acceptance. As you travel through *Humbug to Happiness* and you embrace the clarity within this journey, you begin to experience a sense of *hope*—hope in the understanding that you are valued, you are worthwhile, and most importantly, you are deserving of self-love. Further, this journey of understanding is one that every individual must take. Once you have reached your journey's end, you *will* have an increased sense of feeling *at home*.

Home is knowing. Knowing your mind, knowing your heart, knowing your courage.

—The Wizard of Oz

You have always had the power...[You] just had to learn it for [your]self.

—The Wizard of Oz

Groundhog Day

Ever wonder why...

You seem to get into the same types of relationships over and over and over again?

When you begin to experience the climb of success, it always seems to come crashing down?

You seem to be stuck in the cycle of addiction?

You seem to struggle with your weight?

You seem to struggle with your emotions?

You seem to have thoughts that you are just not pretty enough, strong enough, or smart enough?

M y friend, if you have answered yes to any of the questions listed on the previous page, this book has been delivered to you by your asking. In your search for help, you are aware of your internal chaos and seek freedom from it. As your heart pounds with uncertainty, don't be frightened, as you are not alone. Right now, as you hold your Kindle, iPad, or book in your hand, slowly gaze up from the page you are on. As your eyes gaze beyond the binding that secures the pages of this book of reclamation, look around you. As you contemplate the horizon, what you believe you see at first glance in scanning the environment are individuals with confidence and assuredness as they move about. Although there may be individuals who have established a strong sense of self, there are far more individuals who suffer from their current false perceptions as they ruminate over their own questions that slowly decay their own sense of self and worthiness.

Humbug to Happiness is here to assist you in understanding that if your perception of those who appear to have it all together is potentially incorrect, could your perspective about how you have seen yourself up to this point also be incorrect?

The message within *Humbug to Happiness* is to assist you in understanding that your perspective, vision, or frame of reference has been adulterated by your life story—a life story that was penned during your early development by the negative verbal and nonverbal *humbug* messages absorbed and inked on the tabula rasa, or blank slate, that is your brain. The people you see beyond the page, the people you work with on a day-to-day basis, and even the stranger in front of you in line at your favorite coffee shop—I can say with a great deal of certainty that you share an affinity with more of these individuals than you allow yourself to believe.

This book has been delivered to you by your asking. In searching for help, you are aware of your internal pain and seek to find freedom from it. For most, the pain associated with the answers to the inquiry above sits deep within the *core* of their being. Having been unable to find release from their pain, many search out unhealthy and destructive patterns of behavior to anesthetize their inner wounds in hope of seeking relief. The numbing elixir for the pain is delivered in many forms. Some individuals choose concoctions to deaden the pain such as food, sex, work, alcohol, or drugs. The list of antidotes used for the primary purpose of emotional numbing is certainly endless. There are numerous sources that engender the unique trickery of the humbug messages of our past, provoking the internal pain. Sources that include; members from our own family, acquaintances to our closest and dearest friends. Similarly, there are also myriad methods to deaden the internal pain. All this is done so painstakingly to avoid discovering the true potential of the gift that lies deep within.

This book will provide you the freedom you have been tirelessly searching for. *Humbug to Happiness* will provide you with the understanding of how you have become hypnotized by this cycle of living—specifically, how your brain creates a neural network that contains habituated patterns of thought. These patterns of thought then lead to the development of a unique set of *root* beliefs connected to how you identify yourself. Further, how you have come to identify yourself has kept you entrenched in a frozen time loop of your past, birthed from the messages that swirled around you during your early development.

This recurring time loop of your experience can be likened to that of the characters in the 1993 movie *Groundhog Day*, with Bill Murray and Andie MacDowell. The main character, Phil Connors, is played by Bill Murray. The comedy woven into the script of *Groundhog Day* is brought to life as Phil finds himself stuck in the exasperating rut of reliving his discontentment from feeling underappreciated or undervalued as a news reporter. Specifically, Phil is distraught that his skill as a reporter has been denigrated by him being assigned to report on the harbinger of winter—the groundhog, Punxsutawney Phil. This seemingly trivial assignment will unravel the core of Phil's understanding of his purpose. More importantly, Phil is awakened to how his purpose is part of the grander scheme of the microcosm that is Punxsutawney, Pennsylvania.

Like Phil, many of us live hypnotized by the indignation of our past by reliving it in the present. The reliving of this cycle is often an irritation that pulsates in the present from our resentment, fear, rejection, disappointment, and feelings of worthlessness rooted in our unconsciousness. In an effort to seek relief from these debilitating emotional states, most of us will lash out at those around us or find ways to numb ourselves from the reality of the pain deep within. These debilitating emotions have been given life through the early humbug messages of our past.

Phil is afforded the opportunity to give up the maladaptive beliefs that had mysteriously kept him bound in the *Groundhog Day* experience of reliving his discontentment. Fortunately, *Humbug to Happiness* can afford you the opportunity to effect change in your life. Unlike Phil's awakening, which was hastened as a requirement from the boundaries of movie length, your awakening and the time lapse therein will be solely determined by your desire and commitment to change your *humbug* beliefs. As Phil did, one must be willing to examine past thoughts, beliefs, and behaviors to bring about change in the present. The character of Phil exemplifies the understanding in *Humbug to Happiness*. Simply put, the message within *Humbug to Happiness* is that your life experiences of the past, rooted in your unconsciousness, have created thoughts and beliefs that lead to the self-fulfilling prophecy of the present.

The lesson for Phil was that he was required to make a conscious decision to act and think differently in the present so that he could be set free from the shackles of the time loop of the past. This shift for Phil begins when he actively begins to make amends to those characters of his past. More importantly, Phil begins to embrace and accept his truth, a truth that identifies his discontentment as a result of his own struggle as a young man. When Phil understands the need for acceptance, he experiences a shift in his thinking. It is only when he grasps this lesson that he begins to accept life on life's terms. The reward and blessings for Phil's awakening was the flowing of all the peace, joy, and love the universe had in store for him.

In the pages of *Humbug to Happiness*, you will be given the tools to awaken from your own time loop of habitual thinking. Additionally, these tools will assist you in overcoming your response to the questions listed above. More importantly, *Humbug to Happiness* will help you to recognize how your resounding response in the affirmative to any of the questions above has engendered the destructive cycle in your life—a cycle that has led to patterns in your life that have left you feeling helpless, hopeless, and numb.

More horrific for some, the cycles encumber and shackle them, leaving many feeling that they are destined to live these patterns over and over again. Sadly, there are many people who will move through the stages of their lives never awakening from their own *Groundhog Day* existences. They will continue to live within the script that holds them captive in the time loop of their banal existence. Once again becoming frustrated, they will question why their lives succumb to the same conclusions time and time again. Unfortunately, freedom for many of them will come only as their bodies are released from the burden of life and the spark of hope is forever at peace for eternity.

This book and its contents are here to offer you the message that *change is possible now*! Further, there are no exclusionary criteria to achieve change. These changes are an offering to anyone, no matter your age, gender, sexual orientation, ethnic background, or economic status. There are no specific requirements related to where you are in your life experience. Whether you are single or divorced, a teacher or student, a law abider or lawbreaker, you hold the key to unlocking the journey required within *Humbug to Happiness*. All that is asked is that you are willing to start the journey with me today. This shared journey will allow us to work together in identifying and unraveling the humbug messages that have bound you in a cycle of self-sabotage throughout your life. The cycle of self-sabotage has hypnotized you to live in a time loop of stagnation.

Once freed from this binding self-sabotage, you will come to recognize your inclination to move toward the miracle that is your true gift. Being drawn to the miracle of your true gift and purpose, you will yield to the understanding of living to your fullest potential.

In recognizing your true potential, you will be eager to reclaim the gift that is you—the gift that, through your life trials and tribulations, you have long since forgotten. *Humbug to Happiness* is meant to help you reestablish your relationship with the miracle of your true self. Further, the journey will assist you in understanding the greater purpose of your gift. More significantly, you will begin to live your life with a revived awareness of your true self. As you come to a greater understanding of your true self, it will bring about a renewal. This will empower you to live to your fullest potential each and every day of your life, without question. You will then begin to embrace the gift that is you, and you will be awakened to the magnificent miracle of your being. This understanding will emanate from you. This emerging awareness will ripple, like a series of waves on the ocean, into the lives of those around you. It will flow into all areas of your life and empower all your relationships. The waves of awareness will bathe your relationships by enveloping them with clarity and nurturing. These relationships will become more conscious. More importantly, the commitment of celebrating your true purpose each and every day will allow others to revel in the opportunity to celebrate their own true purposes.

So let the journey begin!

Humbug Message Exercise: Readiness for Change

Review the Stairs of Change Guide in figure 1. As you review the stairs of change, take time to assess your current commitment to really take the action required to bring about change in your life.

Maintenance

Action—Acts on plan of change

Preparation—Ready to make some changes

Contemplation—Change is needed but not right now.

Precontemplation—Don't see any need for change

Figure 1. The Stairs of Change Guide.

The following questions will assist you in reflecting on why you are here at this moment, searching and searching for an answer to the time loop of your life.

What motivated you to pick up this book?

How badly do you want to change your current life situation?

Are you willing to do what it takes to change?

What will you do today to start change?

Humbug Message Exercise: the Cheers and Jeers of Change

In this exercise, take the time to examine both the cheers and the jeers of choosing to take the journey in *Humbug to Happiness*.

What do your humbug messages tell you that you might lose if you embark on this journey of change? Examples of things you could be at risk of losing include family members, friends, and your old self.

What do your humbug messages tell you about your ability to be successful in this journey?

What humbug message might you hear from your family?

What humbug message might you hear from your friends and associates?

Counteracting the Humbug Message

In this area, list all the *cheers* that will come as a result of taking this journey in *Humbug to Happiness*.

Example: I will feel more empowered!

Assignment: Develop a mantra that echoes your willingness for change.

Example: I am eager, willing, and capable of embracing change today!

1.   Write the mantra on several index cards.
2.   Place the index cards in various places you find yourself throughout the day (mirror, nightstand, door, car, and desk).
3.   Read the mantra each time you see the index card.
4.   When reading the mantra, deliberately breathe in each letter and word as though you were drinking it like a glass of water.
5.   Allow yourself the time to quench your thirst for change as you read the message.

Patience and Fortitude

My friends, I am about to broach a subject that many of us look at with trepidation. Don't let it intimidate you, as the subject matter is not unfamiliar to many who have been on a journey of self-discovery. The content within this book has been discussed throughout history by a number of people in many ways. I give much respect and adulation to those who came before me. These harbingers of change encouraged the message of self-awareness embodied by positive thinking and the power of the law of attraction. However, in my own journey and in my journeys as a therapist with others, I felt that a significant piece of our stories was minimized in some of this earlier work. An example of this trivializing is echoed within the message provided by a world-renowned author in the DVD version of the book *The Secret*. (New York 2006)

The author, during his insightful but indifferent discussion, informs us, the viewers, that we are not unique. Further, our lack of uniqueness is rationalized by the author by sharing the message that everyone has the same story. Stories of abuse, neglect, alcoholic parents, and the like appear to be commonplace. In his attempt to connect with the viewer, this successful man shares that his own life story was riddled with similar pain. The impact of our *own* stories is undervalued in a statement during his appearance in the DVD version of the Secret. A statement that says, "So what? Just get over it."

This is where I believe most self-help pioneers have missed the mark. The act of minimizing or trivializing the stories of abuse or neglect of an individual's past by simply saying, "So what?" or "Get over it," reaches a level of callousness that likens itself to the abuse cycle of a perpetrator. The perpetrators or the nonbelievers, in their minimization of their behaviors, render a child/adolescent a victim and insignificant. In a belittling manner, it suggests that what happened to a victim is not important. Even more disheartening for a victim, it reaffirms the humbug messages lodged deep within the tabula rasa. These humbug messages say, "I am not worthy, I am not deserving, I am not protected, and I am not a gift to the universe." This breathes life to a destructive cycle of thought—one that will be etched deeply within the unconscious.

The work within *Humbug to Happiness* will go beyond what has come before. *Humbug to Happiness* will provide an opportunity for lifelong change, should you decide to invest in the journey. It's a journey in which your history will be revealed. In revealing your history, you will come to a greater understanding of why happiness seems so elusive for you. *Humbug to Happiness* will take great care and sensitivity to address your past so that you can be set free from it.

An essential component to your lifelong change is the willingness to understand the history behind your stories. These stories are what have laid the foundation of your belief structure of self. I am here to help you, the reader recognize that your particular story of growth and development as an individual is significant. In taking the time to understand your history, together we will become familiar with your habituated thinking patterns. In choosing to take the necessary time to unravel your habituated thinking patterns, you can truly be successful in changing the course of your life, starting now. In your willingness to dive deep into the unconscious layers of your thinking, you will unravel the mysteries of your self-sabotaging and destructive ways. In the unraveling of these mysteries, you will free yourself from what has imprisoned you, liberating you to an increased awareness in understanding the message proclaimed by the law of attraction.

Adults who tell the child within to "Get over it" are, in essence, telling the child within to keep quiet, suck it up, and not feel his or her pain. Moreover, they unknowingly use the same unhealthy tactics, defense mechanisms, and rationalizations that the child within has heard in the past. These tactics from the past are where the humbug message originated. Further, this method continues to neglect the inner child, who is in pain—pain that the inner child yearns to be free from, an internal ache that can only be set free by the willing reflection of the inner child's now transformed shell that is adulthood. A shell that minimizes the pain of the inner child's *humbug messages* of the past with myriad remedies.

It is of utmost importance to understand that it is not my intent to encourage anyone to swim in the cesspool of the humbug messages of his or her past. However, we must unwrap the *root* messages, faulty beliefs, or scripts of the past if we are truly going to be successful in making a change in our lives. It is much more than just thinking differently or positively. If the messages imprinted on your tabula rasa during the pivotal time of your development were that you are unworthy, stupid, ugly, fat, undeserving, or unlovable, how can anyone suggest that an unfamiliar message of positivity could be expected to alter your life?

Can we really expect a woman in her late thirties, who has been struggling with her weight since she was a young girl, to simply begin to think positively as a resolution to her problem? This simply cannot happen with the ease suggested by many authors. It is my contention that for this client to truly achieve success over her life, it would require her to get to the *root* cause or the life script she had been living out over the last several decades of her life. Eventually, her struggle and many others who struggle with their weight would eventually return to their original state of struggle, a cycle that the $20-billion-a-year weight-loss industry anticipates from the more than one hundred million individuals who will find shame in their appearance and begin the cycle of dieting over and over again with diets that range from low calorie, gluten free, low carbohydrate, and all protein, to point counting.

In working with this individual, I came to understand that she had a strong fondness for images and caricatures of pigs. The young woman's predilection for pigs engulfed her home. She had dedicated a special room in her home that she affectionately referred to as the "pigpen." In this special room, images of pigs were hung on the wall with great care. In the kitchen she had salt and pepper shakers, where the seasonings that filled the pot-bellied pigs would gently be released from their snouts.

Again, on the surface this may seem to have little relevance to this client's issues and struggle with her body image. However, I would have you consider this: If we were to use the premise suggested by some authors to simply "Get over it" and think positively, I can say with a great deal of certainty that my client, like many others who struggle with weight, would have limited success in reaching and sustaining a desirable positive image related to her weight.

Please allow me to make it perfectly clear: I have nothing against the diet industry or any other industry that attempts to help those who struggle with body image. However, I would have you, the reader, consider this point. It is not what you are eating; it is what you are *craving* that is the problem. It is my assertion that our hunger comes from the need to fill a void. Further, the hunger is so significant that most experience a deep, internal, constant craving to "feel full" in their lives. It is when we have the illusion of feeling full that we can silence the nagging truth of our inner child. My friends, we must begin uncovering the cause and conditions to what "weighs" us down.

In returning to the story of my client who was pot-bellied-pig friendly, it wasn't until we began to work with her inner child that she was able to truly uncover her affection for pigs. As the client and I continued to work together, she was able to allow herself to listen to her inner child. As she allowed herself the opportunity to return to her childhood, she recalled an interaction with her father. At first glance the interaction with her father seemed to have little significance to the adult shell that sat in front of me. However, it was when she allowed the inner child to speak freely that the impact of the interaction came to light. In listening to the inner child, she shared with me that she felt unloved and rejected by her father. The inner child shared the specific moment in time that the *humbug message* was delivered by her father—more significantly, when the message began to debilitate and numb the little girl.

The inner child says, "My father saw me eating some food off a plate in the kitchen after dinner. After seeing me eat the food off the plate, he said, 'What are you, some kind of human garbage disposal or something?'"

At this time, I would have you consider this question: What might you think of yourself as a little girl or little boy to hear a message from your mother or father who asks, "What are you, a human garbage disposal or something?" Further, I would ask that you delve a little deeper with me into the statement. As a child, what are some of the basic ideas we are taught about pigs? I know for me, some of the messages included pigs are messy, pigs will eat anything, and pigs like to roll around in mud. Now, let's evaluate some statements about human behavior that may be pig-like. Statements like, "Your room looks like a pigsty" or "Don't be such a pig" are some that come quickly to the surface of my memory. How about your ideas of pigs? I would like to emphasize again that it is my deepest belief that oftentimes these *humbug messages* are not delivered with malicious intent. Oftentimes in the hurried and chaotic experience of day-to-day life, many of us can attest to have impulsively spoken words without clear thought of the delivery or the impact they might have on the receiver. I also am not condoning in any way words or messages that are derogatory. It is my fervent belief that it is imperative that we take time to be aware of the choice of words we use toward one another. As I can say with great certainty, most of us have experienced at one time or another being the recipient of words with great power, whether they are good, bad, or neutral. The words will be absorbed by the intended receiver.

In returning to our pigs, our cultural references about pigs are mostly negative. So, it is my fervent belief that my client was unconsciously manifesting the humbug message of her father in her daily life. She was manifesting the message of being a human garbage disposal by surrounding herself with images and caricatures of pigs. Frankly put, pigs were a constant reminder that she was a human garbage disposal. More horrifically, the inner child who looked to her father for approval was belittled and shamed for being pig-like. This humbug message of rejection had become a familiar pattern for my client when looking to be in a relationship—setting herself up to relive the dismissal of her value and worth by her father over and over again. The cycle replays over and over, as though she is caught up in her own *Groundhog Day* experience.

If my client truly wanted recovery from this *Groundhog Day* experience, it would require her to make conscious and deliberate changes in the present. The first suggestion was met with a bit of resistance from my client. The suggestion was to remove any and all pig-related items from her home. I met the resistance of the client with a question that would be the gauge of her true desire for change, a question that can be asked of you when you find you are stuck in your journey from humbug to happiness, a question that will lead to an answer with astonishing impact on your commitment to change. The question asked of my client has origins in reality therapy by William Glasser (California 1991). The question is simply, "How Is what you are doing helping you get what you want?" The answer to this question will provide enlightenment to your willingness to change.

After some discussion, my client eventually acquiesced with a compromise—that all pig-related items from the home would be placed in storage for six months. The second change suggested to my client was the work of forgiveness. In the effort to move forward, my client had to be open to forgive her father for the hurt that was felt by the inner child from his statement. The final suggestion is rooted in the concept of fêng shui. I had asked my client to fill her home environment, work environment, and car with messages that reinforce healthy living, energy, and love. It was of utmost importance that my client begin to populate every aspect of her life with the new messages of change.

Here is a simple exercise that you can do right at this moment. Take a look around at the environment you are in. What kind of lighting fills the room? What kind of artwork or pictures hang on the wall? What kind of sounds surround you as you are in the room or in your car? What kind of olfactory experience are you having? Are there aromas that fill the space with soothing calm and relaxation? Really take a look at your environment. What messages are being absorbed? It is my fervent belief that if you are looking for change, you must commit to a sensory adjustment in all areas of your life. Allow each space you are in to bathe you in the message you most want your life to be filled with.

So, would I have truly served my client by saying, "So what? Just get over it"? Could my client really have sustained permanent change by just thinking positively? For me, the answer is certain, and that is—unequivocally—no. My client required me to meet her and her *inner child* where they were. My client required me to listen to her history. My client required me to take care in providing clear and gentle direction, much like a child in school who is struggling with spelling a word, and in the effort to spell the word correctly, seeks help from his or her teacher. The child is guided by the teacher to look it up in the dictionary.

The problem with this exchange might not be visible on the surface. However, if we look at the situation a little closer, I would like you to consider the following. If the child does not know how to spell the word and he or she reaches out for help, how successful can anyone expect the child to be when searching to find it in the dictionary? The potential result is a frustrated student, who might feel an array of emotions based on already imprinted *humbug messages*, a message that may be echoing that he or she is stupid and incapable. This inner dialogue has the potential to give birth to an irrational thought, such as *I must be perfect or I am a failure*, or *I must do it alone; there is no one who will help me*. The student, just like all of us, needs a gentle hand that provides clear and supportive direction. The example of the struggling student causes me to reminisce.

As I journey back in the corners of my unconscious, I take a nostalgic look back to my days as a student, specifically, my days in high school at Saint Francis de Sales in Toledo, Ohio.

One of the most poignant memories I have from high school is the motto that all freshman Knights learn. The motto is *Suaviter et Fortiter* ("gently and firmly). This is heralded as the cornerstone of my high school's philosophy. This message made such an impression on me as a young freshman entering high school that it has remained with me well beyond my commencement so that I could become the person I am today. In fact, it is a philosophy that I incorporate into all my daily affairs, both personal and professional.

Humbug to Happiness will require you to embrace the philosophy that is the motto of Saint Francis de Sales. The work will require you to move gently and firmly in the direction towards your true purpose. A gentleness with yourself—in understanding that this is a new journey of discovery. A new journey that will require you to move out of your corner of familiarity and complacency. The journey will require you to call upon what you have had all along in this journey that is your life—a firm commitment to change. You are courageous and resilient beyond measure. It has been your firm commitment to discovery your true purpose that has kept you on a path to this point. Whether this path has been good, bad, or indifferent, you have been living the message of the saying "Just keep keepin' on!"

So, gently in manner and firmly in deed (*suaviter et fortiter*), we will embark upon a reprogramming of your thinking. This adjustment in thinking will require deliberate and consistent action that must be taken on your part from this moment forward. Although I wish the journey could be easier, there is no simple answer such as "think positively." To travel from humbug to happiness, we must get to the cause and conditions of our habituated thinking patterns.

The awareness of getting to the cause and conditions is familiar in the program of recovery. Specifically, in the pages of the *Big Book* of the twelve-step program of Alcoholics Anonymous, (New York 2001) there is a clear message that the destructive behavior of alcoholism or drug addiction is but a symptom. Specifically, on page 64, it reads, "Though our decision was a vital and crucial step, it could have little permanent effect unless at once followed by strenuous effort to face, and to be rid of, the things in ourselves that had been blocking us. Our liquor was but a symptom. So WE HAD TO GET DOWN TO THE CAUSES AND CONDITION."

At this point, you may feel you're in a bit of a quandary. After all, you weren't seeking a book on addiction. Further, you may be wondering how a message of recovery can guide you out of the darkness you're experiencing in your life right now; you are not an addict.

In our journey together, I would like you to reconsider how we have come to understand what it is to be an addict. Dictionary.com defines *addiction* as "the state of being enslaved to a habit or practice, or to something that is psychologically or physically habit forming, such as narcotics, to such an extent that its cessation causes trauma." This definition is the one that our culture most supports. Additionally, this definition has been reinforced with the preconceived notion of what an addict or alcoholic looks like. So it is easy for us to distance ourselves from the definition of addiction. Moreover, beliefs such as, *I don't look like an addict, I haven't had any legal problems, I haven't lost anything that is important to me,* or *I haven't needed treatment* keep us further and further from identifying with it.

However, it is my fervent belief that many of us have become addicted to emotional states of being that have left us coiled in confusion throughout our life-span. It's an entanglement that has baffled you up to this moment in your life. It is my assertion that within the definition of addiction there exists at the core the answer that will release us from the spell of the humbug message. The answer, staring right back at us, has been cloaked by the parameters of our culture's definition of addiction. So let's return to the definition of addiction with courage and fearlessly seek what we need to find.

As we examine the definition with more clarity, we may identify with the sense of being enslaved to a habit or practice and may be aware that we have become psychologically addicted. Simply, you may be addicted to a particular humbug message of your past as well as to the emotional state of being that you have been suffering up to this point in your life. These addicted emotional states include resentment, feelings of failure, and thoughts such as *I am unlovable, I am undeserving, I am worthless, I am unable to trust, I am incapable,* and *I am indecisive.* The list goes on.

As you are encapsulated by these emotional states of being, your brain releases chemicals that hook you. Similar to the alcoholic or addict who craves his or her substance, many of us unconsciously crave the release of the chemicals that are naturally released from our brains. These chemicals keep us hooked in the self-degradation of the humbug message and hold us captive from living our true purposes.

Once you consider that the habituated patterns of your life are interwoven with your brain's constant release of natural chemicals that match your thoughts, feelings, and behaviors, you will find some relief. More importantly, there should be a continued sense of relief as you recognize that these are all part of the natural responses that make us the magnificent beings we are. Our brain is constantly releasing chemicals that match our life experiences for future recall. The brain, in its amazing splendor captures all the events of our lives much like a photograph within the neuro-pathways of the brain. These chemically produced photographs within the neuro-pathways can be triggered by our own internal request or external experiences.

So once you embrace that your addiction actually resides in the deception behind the humbug messages of your past, you will experience a quantum leap. Once you recognize this, you will have clarity that your destructive behavior patterns are but a symptom. If this edict is embraced, you will be more willing to accept this proclamation. You have the inherent and astounding ability to change now! You can be empowered and feel renewed and truly find happiness in the gift that is you. However, as it is clearly directed in the journey of recovery, one must get down to the causes and conditions that engendered the symptoms of your destructive thought patterns. These patterns have led you to seek relief through anger, depression, codependency, loneliness, promiscuity, resentment, overeating, gambling, or drug and alcohol addiction. With great fervor, I ask you to consider that it is the false talk of the humbug messages and the natural relationship with the chemical release of the brain that imprint on your tabula rasa during your early development where the cause and conditions breathe. More significantly, these humbug messages have directed your life to this point.

Today can be the beginning of living a life that is full of all the wonderment that was bestowed upon you in the moment of your arrival. Know that there is no one else who can alter this for you. Just like a master sculptor who chips away at the block of marble to create a masterpiece, you, too, must be willing to painstakingly chip away the old layers of the humbug messages. As you continue chipping away the layers, you will uncover the gift of your true purpose.

More importantly, you will recognize that it is the layers of your destructive patterns of thought and behavior that contain the humbug messages of your past. The humbug messages anchor you in the blindness that creates blurred sight to your true purpose. This task is much like the story of Michelangelo. As reported by historians, Michelangelo, while in Rome, very rarely created a sketch of his work when working on any of his masterpieces. Rather, he had a unique philosophy regarding his work. He believed that the masterpiece or its true purpose was already present in the marble. Further, it is said that he would spend hours, sometimes weeks, with the block of marble, as if to listen to the message of the marble's destiny. It was only when he had the clarity of the message that he began to chip away at the block of marble that would become one of his most famous masterpieces, *David*. Michelangelo tirelessly chipped away one of the most magnificent and revered pieces of art of all time from an imperfect block of marble that many sculptors before him rejected. So I say to you, my friend, have patience and fortitude (*suaviter et fortiter*). Let's chip away the layers to reveal the masterpiece that lies within.

Now, before we begin the journey, please allow me to allude to the gratification that this journey is certain to be filled with. It is my contention that the first gift that will be bestowed upon you is a renewed and improved outlook in your relationship with your true self. It is a relationship that so many have cast aside, believing it to be insignificant. In believing it is insignificant, you have continued to minimize the importance of the relationship with your true self. This lessening of self leads to increased neglect of the physical, emotional, and spiritual needs of self as time passes. This neglect leads to an emotional abandonment of self. The abandonment of self leads you to habitual thinking patterns that then lead you to unhealthy behaviors that assist you in the numbing of the sense of emptiness you feel.

Humbug Message Exercise: the Apple Doesn't Fall Far...

In this exercise you will examine your family tree.

Were you raised by both parents?

How did your parents show affection?

What is your birth order?

Did either parent struggle with alcoholism or addiction?

Was there physical, emotional, or sexual abuse?

Who were you closest to? Why?

Who were you told you were just like?

What traits did the person have?

What was expected of you?

What affirming messages did you hear?

What family messages were spoken that you heard growing up? For example: children are to be seen, not heard.

What family messages were not spoken, but behaviors enforced the messages?

Thawing the Gift

The *Humbug to Happiness* journey is grounded in the philosophy that at the very *core* of who you are as an individual is a gift. More importantly, the intention of the *Humbug to Happiness* journey is to awaken you to a level of consciousness that will empower you. In this state of empowerment and awareness, you will fervently reject any message that attempts to minimize the unique miracle of your gift.

The awakening of this gift will require, for some, a willingness to search the depths of their being. Their gifts have lain dormant, much like the imprisoned seeds of spring that lie nestled under the blanket of the frigid winter. Just as winter participates in the act of humbuggery by deceiving us into believing that the beauty of our earth has withered away, the humbug messages of our past deceive us into minimizing our value and purpose. The goal of the humbug message is to deceive us and to make us think that our gift is nonexistent or has passed and will no longer spring forth. Similar to the bitter chill in the subtle winds of winter that whisper in from the north to diminish the beauty of fall, the humbug messages quietly take hold during the early stages of our development. As the bitter-cold humbug messages swirl around us, they begin to freeze the gift of our true purpose.

The gift will continue to lie dormant until we recognize the destructive nature of the humbug messages in our lives. Sadly, there will be those whose knowledge of their true purpose will remain frozen. For some, the act of being fearless in this search for understanding is much too arduous a task. Unfortunately, the unwillingness to uncover one's purpose will yield the same harvest over and over. For those individuals, the bitterness of the chilling humbug messages has provided a reward. Although this reward is negative, it has brought some desired benefit or secondary gain, and the loss of the benefit or secondary gain is too great a cost. The cost of releasing this secondary gain may be that they are no longer able to play the victim. They may lose the freedom of being irresponsible or unaccountable. To them, losing such a reward means, *My family, significant other, and friends won't continue to feel sorry for me or enable me.* For those souls, the loss of the secondary gain would be too devastating. So these individuals will trudge on through the quagmire of their existence, enveloped in apathy. Sadly, these individuals unwittingly decide that the misery is worth it. Unfortunately, we must leave these souls behind until they recognize that they alone hold the key that will set them free from the prison the humbug messages have created.

For those eager to experience a quantum leap in their self-awareness, *Humbug to Happiness* is here to guide them to a greater understanding that they themselves are the masters of the gifts they possess. Further, they will recognize that at their birth, they were intended to come to an awareness of their gifts. More importantly, they are meant to share that gift with the world.

Many of us, however, shuffle along on the frozen, superficial surface. We are led by the frigid deception the humbug messages have imprinted within the neurological pathways of the brain. The development of the brain has been discussed throughout history by many of the great philosophers and thinkers. *Humbug to Happiness* describes the brain as a tabula rasa, or blank slate. During various stages of our development, we experience external and internal sensory messages that lay the foundation of our understanding of self. These sensory experiences are made up of the good, the bad, and the ugly of our life and rest in the unconscious brain. These sensory experiences occur throughout our early development. Further, these sensory messages can be delivered with both purposeful intentions and unintentional ignorance.

The delivery of these humbug messages is materialized by myriad sources. These sources come to us from the inner circle of our family to the outermost circle of peers and the culture we live in. The concept of tabula rasa is described in Book III, Chapter 4, of what is probably the first textbook on psychology: *De Anima*, or *On the Soul*, by Aristotle (New York 2007). In *De Anima*, Aristotle postulates that the brain is an uninscribed tablet or blank slate. Additionally, the concept of the brain as a tabula rasa is discussed in the modern writings of John Locke. In his essay, "Concerning Human Understanding in the Seventeenth Century," Locke said, "The mind is, at birth, a blank slate without rules for processing."(New York 1939) The debate concerning brain development continues to intrigue researchers to this day.

As technology makes advancements in neuroimaging, the ability to understand the intricate details of the brain has emerged. We now understand that at birth we are equipped with almost all the neurons we will require.

In short, what we know is that the brain, in its splendid design, is the harbinger of both our magnificent sense of self and the disparaging messages of unworthiness and the like. Our journey in *Humbug to Happiness* will take us deeper into the brain in the chapter titled "If I Only Had A..."

Again, internal and external sensory experiences create the neural pathways and imprint the humbug messages on the tabula rasa, or blank slate. The internal and external experiences envelop every aspect of our understanding of self. More significantly, they come to define numerous aspects of our sense of self, both the positive and negative perceptions that guide our life.

The sources of these internal and external sensory experiences range from the most reprehensible, such as sexual or physical abuse, to what is perceived as less heinous—emotional or verbal abuse. Often, the stealthy and covert emotional and verbal abuse can be just as insidious and damaging to the miracle of a child's gift as physical or sexual abuse. It is necessary at this time to understand that *all* traumas affect our development to some degree. In understanding this premise, *Humbug to Happiness* will attempt to provide healing to *all* levels of *trauma* that may have been experienced.

Our culture, although improving, has a tendency to minimize the impact of emotional or verbal abuse, as the bruises and scrapes are not so visible. However, so deceiving is this manner of abuse that most individuals struggle or are unable to make the connection back to their childhood or adolescence. So, under the spell of the deception and trickery of the humbug message, many are unable or unwilling to fathom that anything of this nature ever occurred at all. Certainly this can be said for all levels of trauma. The deception and trickery of the humbug message make most of us move on in our lives, numb from the chilling humbug messages and feeling perplexed. More often than not, many continue to grapple with why their lives seem to always end up the way they do.

The trepidation is a result of the humbug messages that will almost always debilitate us. We are trapped by the humbug messages as they ever so delicately imprint on our tabula rasa. As these messages imprint, our thinking patterns become more entrenched; they become a network of thought. This network of thought leads to the creation of a pattern in the neural pathways of our brain, which in turn, creates the personal beliefs we have of ourselves and the world.

Like the snow covering the ground, these subtle verbal and nonverbal humbug messages blanket us and prevent us from understanding and celebrating our own uniqueness. More insidiously, the deception will freeze our hopes and our dreams and imprison us all the days of our lives. Today this book is delivered to you to share the great news. Simply put, you can break free from the grip of the humbug messages. You can finally set yourself free from the deception that has fettered you to the habitual patterns of your behavior. These behaviors include alcohol and drug use, overeating, unhealthy relationships, promiscuity, gambling, emotional explosiveness, and other destructive patterns. You will truly be setting yourself free so that you can fully live the purpose of your gift that you were meant to share with the world. More importantly, you will set yourself free to embrace and celebrate the gift in a world of love, happiness, and contentment for the rest of your days.

However, to release yourself from the frozen grip of these humbug messages, you will be required to use the HOW method of change. This journey will require you to make a personal commitment to be *honest* with yourself, *open* to the suggestions within this book, and *willing* to make an effort to practice change. But more importantly, what will be required of you is something that most people who know success and happiness understand so well. Successful people know that the secret to change and success is deeply correlated with their willingness to have an unwavering dedication to *take action* on a daily basis. Your success and happiness in life will be equal to the unwavering dedication you have to change.

Frankly, when you invest in yourself 100 percent, without question, your return will be the same. However, failure to invest 100 percent in yourself will keep you entrenched in the same cycle that you are most familiar with, day after day and year after year. My hope is that at this moment, the day this book called to you in response to your searching, you are ready to invest 100 percent in yourself! More significantly, my hope is that you are energized with an unwavering dedication to revealing your true purpose so that you can experience the miracle that is you. Once you relearn your true purpose, you will celebrate the rewards and blessings of this knowledge from this day forward.

If you choose this fantastical journey today, you cannot use any more excuses such as, "I will get to this tomorrow" or "I have tried so many other times, and it never works." It is my declaration that this book will assist you in thawing the depths of the humbug messages that have rooted you in guilt, shame, and denial of the gift that is you. But more importantly, this journey will allow you to feel empowered and to embrace the true gift that is you, allowing you to celebrate the miracle that you truly are. It is my hope that you allow this book to empower you and encourage you to be the master sculptor of the gift that is you. During your journey within *Humbug to Happiness*, you will be encouraged to reinvest in the most significant gift the world has known, which was bestowed upon you during the miracle of your arrival. It is the gift of knowing the pure essence of who you are, the gift of self—the gift of *love*. This gift can only be reawakened and brought forth if you are willing to open the heart and mind of your inner child. It is your inner child that yearns for you to return to the pure essence of your being. It is your inner child who guards the gift that is your birthright.

Humbug to Happiness Exercise: Thawing the Gift

As the adult shell silences the gift that is the inner child, we often forget those things that filled our inner child's eyes with awe. In this exercise, allow yourself to go back to a time when your inner child danced as if no one was watching, sang like no one could hear, and lived fully each and every day.

Who was your best friend?

What was your favorite food?

What was your most favorite Christmas gift?

What birthday do you remember most?

Did you have a favorite pet?

What was your favorite color?

What was your favorite cartoon show?

What was your favorite candy?

What was your favorite game to play in your neighborhood?

What was your favorite thing to daydream about?

Who was your favorite teacher?

Who was your best friend in school?

What was the coolest thing you and a friend ever did?

What did you want to be when you grew up?

What was your favorite ice cream?

What was your favorite dessert growing up?

What song did you like to sing?

Who was your favorite music group or singer?

Who was your favorite superhero?

What was your favorite poster?

What was your favorite movie growing up?

Deception at Work

amily and friends have asked why I decided on the title *Humbug to Happiness*. The reason for their inquisitiveness was twofold. Their first concern was that the word *humbug* is an unfamiliar, old-fashioned, stale, and out-of-date word. The second concern that plagued them was whether this antiquated word would resonate with our culture today. While their concern with the word *humbug* may be accurate, it is my claim that the word *humbug*, as defined by the dictionary, aligns perfectly with the journey we will embark upon together. In the sharing of this journey together, we will traverse through the minefield of the humbug messages of the past with a course set for the final port of call: happiness.

Humbug, as defined by *Merriam-Webster*, is "language or behavior that is false or meant to deceive people." Further, it is defined as "someone or something that is not honest or true." I eagerly request that you embrace this definition, as it is imperative in the recovery of self. We must see these humbug messages as they truly are. They are messages that are false. Humbug messages are typically delivered by individuals who, through their own lack of knowing themselves, feel a sense of inadequacy or disappointment. Overwhelmed with their current states, they subconsciously feel they must protect themselves from withering away to the nothingness and emptiness that guts them.

In recognizing the goal of this journey, I believe that the core definition of *humbug* describes perfectly the art and skill that are woven into the assumed benign cloak of the humbug messages. More insidious is the stealth power that the humbug messages have on the receiver once the message is conveyed. The powerful imprint of the misguided and fraudulent message hidden within the humbug chastisement is absorbed as part of the existing neural pathway of the receiver.

The receiver does not determine freely the gravity or impact of the conveyed humbug message. The receiver is incapable of qualifying the gravity or impact of the humbug message, whether it has been delivered by a parent, teacher, coach, sibling, peer, or the current culture. However, the message begins to fuel the sense of self.

Now, before the critics begin to cry foul, I think it is imperative that I share my belief that often the humbug message is *not* intentionally delivered with malicious intent by someone's parent, peers, or society. Rather, it is created by many from ignorance of their own habituated patterns of thought that have innocuously etched a *core* belief that lies within their own damaged senses of self, waiting in the subconscious.

The release of the humbug message typically stirs when either an internal or external force fuels an individual's core belief. The core belief, much like a fire pit, continues to be fed by the fanning of these internal and external embers. The core belief is then ignited and fires the already established neural pathways of the brain. Once the neural pathways have ignited, the pathways begin to instigate the core beliefs that may be connected to the sense of failure, inadequacy, rejection, insecurity, or worthlessness. The core belief then inundates the individual with thoughts that have developed a relationship connected to the familiar pain of these humbug messages. As the thoughts flood the neural pathways of the brain, the emotions connected to the experience are triggered. As they experience the emotions, most individuals will lash out. This is for the sole purpose of protecting their egos and sense of self. Unfortunately, in the effort to protect their sense of self from the wounds of their humbug messages, they inadvertently erode the sense of self of those they love. This becomes a dance that perpetuates the vicious cycle that so many continue to subconsciously engage in from generation to generation.

During my career as a teacher and counselor, spanning twenty-plus years, I became cognizant of the significant erosion that these humbug messages have had. More importantly, I have come to understand how the humbug messages that have been delivered throughout people's life-spans infiltrate the core of their internal sense of self at a deeper level of cognition than most are willing to embrace. My awareness of this impact has been fueled by the stories of the many men, women, and children who graciously allowed their inner children to speak their stories of pain freely to me over the last twenty years. It is in the sharing of their stories that I felt compelled to step out of my comfort zone to provide more to the world, as it is my contention that we are all connected. More significantly, we are all called to step out of our own comfort zones and do more to bring about change in the world.

The concept of stepping out of one's own comfort zone and realizing one's own fullest potential is rooted in many theories of the past. In his book, *The Organism: A Holistic Approach to Biology Derived from Pathological Data in Man* (New York: Batan Books,1939), Kurt Goldstein shares that "every individual, every plant, every animal has only one inborn goal—to actualize itself." In a similar message, Abraham Maslow purports, through his hierarchy of needs, that we are all driven toward self-actualization. However, one must successfully achieve grappling with the lower-level needs, such as the physiological needs, in order to continue the momentum toward self-actualization. Further, Abraham Maslow's article, "A Theory of Human Motivation," is where he clearly defines self-actualization to be "the desire for self-fulfillment, namely the tendency for an individual to become actualized in what he/she is potentially."

The hierarchy of needs suggested by Abraham Maslow:

Self-
Actualization
Esteem Needs
Love and Belonging
The Safety Needs
The Physiological Needs

Figure 2. Maslow's Hierarchy of Needs.

Maslow attempts to provide some guidance on the characteristics that are common among those individuals working toward self-actualization. These characteristics include:

1. **Acceptance and realism.** It is Maslow's contention that self-actualized individuals have a realistic perception of themselves, others, and the world they live in.
2. **Problem centering.** Maslow suggests that self-actualized individuals are concerned with solving problems outside themselves, including assisting others and finding solutions for world problems. He further suggests that these individuals are typically motivated by their sense of responsibility and ethics.
3. **Spontaneity.** Maslow suggests that self-actualized individuals are spontaneous in their inward thoughts and outward behaviors. While understanding the need to conform to rules and social expectations, they move toward being open and unconventional.
4. **Autonomy and solitude.** It is here that the self-actualized individual understands the significance of independence and privacy. Although the self-actualized person enjoys the company of others, he or she understands the need to focus on developing his or her own individual potential.
5. **Continued freshness of appreciation.** The self-actualized individual is one who tends to view the world with appreciation, wonder, and awe. Self-actualized individuals have an understanding that even simple experiences can be a source of inspiration and pleasure for them.

The message that ripples through *Humbug to Happiness* is that one must successfully acquire the essential skill set within the hierarchy to become fully self-actualized. Let's begin the journey up the hierarchy of needs. Calling on my time as a fifth-grade teacher, we will examine the lower-level needs. These lower-level needs include food, water, and shelter. The significance of Maslow's hierarchy of needs is present at the start of each school day. If a child leaves home without having had some form of breakfast, that child will not perform to his or her fullest potential. The basic need of hunger renders the child unable to focus on the task at hand. Certainly, the need to satisfy hunger and thirst is applicable to many of us who need a cup of coffee to start the day.

Once the basic needs of hunger and thirst are addressed, we become more equipped to focus on the current task at hand. Essentially, the theory can be likened to a ladder. Would you purchase a ladder missing the two bottom rungs? You may think the query is rather silly, but I ask you to consider this: If the bottom rungs were missing, wouldn't your task of reaching the top pose some difficulty? How about the journey down? Can it be done? Absolutely. However, it will impede your ability to complete the task in the most efficient manner.

Returning to the hierarchy of needs, let's inspect the next "rung" suggested by Maslow. Maslow describes the next "rung" as the need for safety. It is my belief that at this level, many individuals experience their initial internal struggles with their sense of self.

It is here at the most poignant times of our lives, our births, when safety begins to actively influence our gift. When we are infants, it is the mother or primary caretaker who provides all our needs. These include feeding, soothing, and the development of attachment.

It is the behavior of the mother or primary caretaker that develops attachment or lack thereof. However, our need for a sense of safety doesn't end after we no longer require a bottle. The need for a sense of safety continues as the child begins to explore the world. There is comfort and security in knowing that Mommy and Daddy are right there if I need them when something goes awry. The imprinting of a sense of security and safety is also played out in a familiar game played by mothers or primary caretakers—the game of peekaboo! Many may not fully understand the value of this often silly and giggle-producing exercise. This simple game of peekaboo is actually rooted in an essential life lesson for children—the child becomes aware that there are times that the caretaker is gone but will be back.

I ask you to consider this: How might a child's sense of security be affected if he or she is uncertain on any given day that Mommy or Daddy will be back? Further, as Maslow suggests, the hierarchy of needs is fluid. Simply put, we may experience issues with these needs at various times during our life-spans. Let's take, for example, the horrific housing debacle of several years ago. I can say with certainty that many mothers and fathers saw the ominous dark cloud of losing their home looming over them, which created disruptions in their psyches as well as in their everyday lives. Hence, they experienced a lack of security not only for themselves but for their families as well.

Questions to Ponder

Do we really believe, as a culture, that children are impervious to the issues of divorce aftermath?

Do we really believe that a child is immune to the toxicity of an addicted home?

Can we really minimize the long-term impact that physical, verbal, emotional, and sexual abuse have in developing a sense of security or belonging?

Can we really stand by the idea that TV, video games, and music don't have an impact on our developing minds?

Humbug Scenario I

A young man in his early twenties recounts living in an environment where an alcoholic mother would be gone for days or sometimes weeks at a time. He describes being filled with such anxiety on a daily basis as he and his siblings would board the school bus. The young man was riddled with anxiety that was rooted in the fear of not knowing whether his mother would be home when he returned.

Let's return to the playful life skill of peekaboo.

The young man's sensory suite had absorbed both the internal and external humbug messages of his life experience. Further, the absorbed experience became etched on the tabula rasa of this young boy, resting in his unconscious until awakened or triggered. It is the sense of security in the hierarchy of needs that affects this young man today. The lack of security in the young man's childhood affects the way he interacts in relationships now. Moreover, it affects his ability to trust anyone significant in his life, for fear that they will leave. So the young man overcompensates in his relationships while neglecting his feelings.

Humbug Scenario II

I had the pleasure of meeting and working with a young man in his early twenties while he was waiting to be sentenced for burglary. Since this was not his first time committing such a crime, he was being charged as a habitual offender. As I spent time with this young man, I became intrigued by his history of taking from others. As I met with him and listened to his inner child's story, it brought clarity about why the young man's belief was "When I want something of yours, I have the right to take it."

The young man's story begins with a single mother, who struggled to make ends meet. In an effort to lighten her financial woes, she moved in with a male friend she had known for some time. His mother got the young man to the front of the house for the bus as she made her way to work. Her male friend would then have the young boy come back to the house. The young man was instructed to perform oral sex on the man.

This story made such an impact on me that I presented this young man's story as part of a presentation to a group of two-hundred-plus officers and lawyers. First, I shared that I certainly did not condone the behavior of stealing. Moreover, I believe that there should be consequences for his behavior. However, I asked them, as I will ask you, to consider this question: If someone's actions have demonstrated that he or she can take or do something without consequences, wouldn't we expect this message to create behavior exactly like the incarcerated young man's? That is a core message that says, "What is yours is mine. I should be able to take what is yours when I want it, without asking." Again, at the very core, we are looking at the absence of a sense of security or safety for this young man as a child.

Humbug Message Exercise: My Safety Needs

Figure 3. Maslow's Hierarchy of Needs.

Looking at the hierarchy of needs in figure 3, take the time to answer these questions related to a sense of safety and security.

1. Did you feel safe in your home?
2. Did you feel safe around family members?
3. Where did you feel the most safe and secure?
4. When you were hurt, was there someone there to provide comfort to you?
5. If someone hurt you, did your parents believe you when you shared it with them?
6. When did you feel most unsure of your safety?
7. Do you worry when you are in a relationship that the other person may leave?

I must be forthcoming at this point. It is vital that you recognize that there are no quick routes to becoming self-aware or self-actualized. *Humbug to Happiness* will require every participant to recognize the roadblocks that have been creating the chains that shackle them. More importantly, these roadblocks hold them imprisoned, preventing them from achieving their highest potential. I can say with conviction that for most individuals who asked for this journey, the emptiness or void that called out for understanding is the result of a particular need that has not been met. It is an essential part of your growth that yearns to be addressed. If the premise of self-actualization is accurate, which I believe it is, once you become victorious in filling the chasm of your emptiness, you will naturally seek to grow into who you are—one who is self-actualized.

In my agreement with my higher power to pay it forward, *Humbug to Happiness* will continue to revisit the stories of amazing individuals who have molded me into the counselor and teacher I am today. More significantly, it is their willingness to share their stories that continually inspires me to be a better man in a world where so many individuals' inner children yearn to be heard. The inner child is simply looking to have a sense of security and belonging. Most importantly, an inner child is looking to be loved.

It is my belief that the humbug messages are delivered and carried out as if by a magician's sleight of hand. This sleight of hand often involves the observer being humbugged by the many distraction tactics of the magician. Moreover, the sleight of hand is intended to make a movement appear as though what has occurred is ordinary and completely innocent. However, the sleight of hand is a hoax intended to distract the observer. This manipulates the observer by misdirecting the observer's attention. So important to the magician, the sleight of hand has seven principles as described by the magicians Penn and Teller.

For one to truly understand how magic continues to amaze millions all over the world, it is imperative to understand how the brain works. Once we understand the relationship between our brains and the magician's sleight of hand, we will be more cognizant of the hoax or deception. Or will we?

As David Strayer, a psychologist and researcher from the University of Utah, has indicated, (Burglington 2011) our brain can only truly ever concentrate on one thing at a time. Further, he shares that although we attempt to convince ourselves that we are multitasking, the fact is that we are merely shifting our attention from one task to another. So the art of the magician continues to keep us entertained. However, the magician's true assistant in the humbuggery is our own brain. It is my contention that you will discover within *Humbug to Happiness* that the brain, by its nature, is an unwitting participant in the deceptive humbug messages that burden and hold many captive all the days of their lives.

Forging the Links, Yard by Yard

or me, *Humbug to Happiness* is a reflection of the unique and memorable journey of two very different men. At first glance, they appear to be different in time and character. The reflection of the inner turmoil is the affinity they share. However, it is in the arduous task of their journey of reclamation that both men will find electrifying joy in the rest of their days.

Humbug to Happiness is reminiscent of the fantastical journey of reclamation for a crotchety old man, found in the pages of Charles Dickens's *A Christmas Carol*. The spirits of Christmas past, present, and future bestow the journey of renewal upon the miserly old man Ebenezer Scrooge.

These specters are all invested in facilitating an expedition for Scrooge. This journey is presented to Scrooge so that he may know transformation and recovery from the desolate existence of a man of the worldly mind. It is the apparition of his deceased friend Jacob Marley, who offers Scrooge the daunting foreshadowing of what is to come should he maintain the "bah humbug" attitude of his current reality. I believe that Jacob Marley offers the first glimpse of the law of attraction. Marley delivers the resonating message to Scrooge. He has disdain for Scrooge's ignorance and curiosity about the specter's chains.

"You are fettered," said Scrooge, trembling. "Tell me why?"

"I wear the chain I forged in life," replied the ghost. "I made it link by link and yard by yard; I girded it on of my own free will, and of my own free will, I wore it."

Marley, in his death, offers to Scrooge the gift of understanding his life lessons. Marley says, "I am here tonight to warn you that you have yet a chance and hope of escaping my fate."

Transfixed by the apparition, Scrooge eventually heeds the warning. However, as the ghost of Marley slowly fades into the eternal wasteland of burdened souls roaming the earth, Scrooge once again falls victim to his humbug ways. Hypnotized by his habitual "bah humbug" mentality, Scrooge minimizes Marley's visit. He returns to the familiar self-loathing that pacifies his isolation from the cruel world outside his chamber. This loathing leads him to retreat deeper into the internal chamber of his resentments and fears.

Much like Scrooge, when some people are afforded the opportunity of reclamation, they will retreat to their inner Ebenezer and echo, "Bah humbug." For those of you who do so, I am here to assist you in understanding that, just like Ebenezer, your belief that such an opportunity is a hoax is simply rooted in fear. This fear may have some foundation in reality. It was created as a result of the multiple times you have reached for that glimmer of hope only to have it snuffed out by the haunting "bah humbug" messages of your habituated life. Humbug messages have kept you fettered to the familiar cycle of your life.

Dickens, in his magical story of reclamation, is not only the harbinger of the law of attraction. I believe Dickens is also foreshadowing the tenets of inner-child work. The precepts that are vital to inner-child work today are alluded to by the Ghost of Christmas Past. The ghost offers both Scrooge and his audience a glimpse of a child's past, nestled in the unconscious mind of the resentment-filled, crotchety old man. He is a man who exclaims, "Bah humbug" to the messages of love, kindness, and merriment.

Before we move further in examining the underlying tenets within Dickens's writings, I must ask of you what Charles Dickens requested of his readers—as well as his

Figure 4. Breaking the Links.

audiences, as he performed his one-man show, *A Christmas Carol*—regarding his labor of love in 1843. The cornerstone of his beloved story requires a willingness to emphatically understand and accept as truth that Jacob Marley's death is certain. If Marley's death were not distinctly understood, nothing wonderful would come of the story he was going to relate. It is in the understanding that Marley was "dead as a doornail" that the miracle of reclamation is built upon. So for something wonderful to come of this story within *Humbug to Happiness*, I must request that you accept these three truths that must be distinctly understood: your inner child seeks to be heard, yearns to be understood, and requires you to listen to its messages deep within your unconscious.

Let's travel with Scrooge and the Ghost of Christmas Past to where a child sits alone and neglected. He has no friends but that of the beloved characters within the books he reads. The child is alone on Christmas Day, deserted by family and friends. His father holds a grudge against him because his wife died during the child's birth. As Scrooge begins to reflect, the specter pleads, "Weep for the boy, if the tears will come."

It is in Scrooge's continued journey with the Ghost of Christmas Past that we get a glimpse of how the young child, once deserted and neglected, becomes a man who feels undeserving of love and attachment—a man who echoes the inner child's pain when he is left in a cold, dark, and strange place by the specter of Christmas Present. Scrooge, sitting alone, appeals to the already departed spirit of Christmas Present to return. As his cry goes unheard, Scrooge returns to his familiar behavior of withdrawing. Scrooge is left alone to sit once again, deserted and neglected.

Scrooge, wrought with his fears of being alone, asks, "What have I done to be abandoned like this?" It is in this final journey with Christmas Present that we are given the glimpse of the tenets of inner-child work. Scrooge, as he lifts his eyes to the dark and empty sky, appeals for an answer to the question that anchors the inner child in his loneliness. His father was shackled by his own mourning at the loss of his wife during childbirth and unwittingly cast a humbug message on young Scrooge. This was surreptitiously imprinted on the tabula rasa of the young boy.

This relationship with his father infiltrates Scrooge's sense of worth throughout his travels with the specter. More significantly, we see how all Scrooge's relationships are rooted in the pain of the child that he once was. He was a child neglected, deserted, and alone, who later becomes a crotchety old man. The old man builds walls that muffle the painful messages of the inner child, who suffers from being unheard. However, the crotchety old man can be set free from the pain of the past if he elects to receive the message of renewal from the Ghost of Christmas Past.

In taking a slight detour from our story of Scrooge and his passage to his truth—a truth that begins to reveal the origins of his inner angst of "bah humbug," I begin to reflect on one of the most noteworthy experiences in my adult life, an experience so profound that as the memories cascade into my consciousness, my eyes begin to well with tears, tears that now bring solace as I share my story, a comfort found in the tears as a result of being afforded the opportunity to have had the experience prior to my father's passing. Although my journey lacks the supervision of a specter, it mirrors the journey Scrooge shared with the spirit of Christmas past.

So journey back with me to my past, not long past, but my past, where as a young man of twenty-six, I sat ruminating in the backseat of my parents' maroon Buick Park

Avenue. I was a young man bursting with my early acumen on my academic journey in psychology, and sitting in the backseat of the car, I ruminated over the necessity of addressing the query that rattled deep within my own tabula rasa, a question that echoed from the early imprinting within the unconscious that beleaguered my own inner child, a query from the inner child that solicited a resolution.

Sitting anxiously in the backseat of the car during the first hour of the drive, the internal tension of discomfort was palpable. The dis-ease and tension was so great that the windows in the car became fogged with moisture. My dis-ease increased as I evaluated the consequences of my actions should I follow through with them, and I debated whether the inquiry would be so damaging that it would cause a disruption in my relationship with my parents. Summoning up the courage in the second hour of our adventure, I spoke up.

As my voice trembled, I spoke these words, "Mom and Dad, I have a question to ask both of you. I know it may be uncomfortable, but I have to ask it. I have to ask, why don't we say 'I love you' to each other as a family? Or offer hugs of encouragement?"

After some pause and feeling the discomfort of the silence, I spoke up again, saying, "I mean, I'm sure you love all your children, but I don't think I have ever heard it said."

My mother and father, speaking almost in unison, said, "Of course we love our children. With all that we have done for all of you, how could you ask that?"

Feeling the undercurrent of shame, I said, "I know that you have done many things for all your children, but I guess I'm saying I would like to hear you say it." Further, I was providing an out by indicating to my parents, "Hey, even if you don't mean it, I just want to know that you can say the words."

My father, a man of few words, gazed into the rearview mirror. His eyes, contemplating the backseat of the car, searched out my presence. In finding me, my father, making certain our eyes connected, spoke words that rippled in the car like an electric charge, a charge that surged through all my senses. Keeping connection with my father's eyes as if to prepare for what was to come as he spoke, I felt a surge fill my heart.

My father said, "David, I know that we don't say it enough; I know I don't say it, and I wish we would say it more." My father, his gaze still locked, continued by saying, "Know that I love you, David."

With tear-filled eyes, I said, "Thank you for saying it. I know that it may have been hard to do, but know that I love you, Dad. Hearing you say those words means so much."

The emotional charge that had filled the space of the car slowly began to wane as the discomfort of the question continued to burden my mother while she sat quietly in the front passenger seat of the car. In returning to my parents' home, we spoke of the enjoyment the family could share if we decided to purchase the summer cottage. Having completed the journey to investigate the summer cottage, I informed my parents I was going to walk home. Searching out my mother before I left, I found her in the kitchen.

As I approached the kitchen, my mother asked, "Do you want to stay and have something to eat?" I shared that I had already eaten prior to the trip and thanked her. As I began to step out of the kitchen, my mother whispered, "You know I love you, right?"

I said, "Mom, I have always known you love me by your actions, but it feels so good to hear you say it." Opening my arms to hug her, I said, "I know that this was hardest for you, but know that I love you, too."

It was on my walk home that evening that I realized two things extremely important in order for me to understand my parents. Further, these things must be understood in your journey within *Humbug to Happiness*.

First, I needed to understand that each of my parents had his or her own comfort zone in which my mother or my father could feel safe in order to become vulnerable. My mother's safe zone was her kitchen. My mother is and always has been a mother who loved to "feed" those she loved. As her son, I had to understand that in a moment of being vulnerable, she felt safest in her kitchen. Second, I had to come to the understanding that parents do the very best they can with the resources they have in raising their children. Their parenting skills, for the most part, are a reflection of how they were raised by their parents.

So, similar to my life experience above, this journey is one that is yours to freely take, the same way it was for Scrooge. So I ask you at this time to breathe in courage and release doubt based on what you have tried in the past. I encourage you to breathe in and have unwavering faith that change is possible. I am here to tell you that it is okay to be filled with some hesitation, just as Scrooge initially struggled to accept the message from Marley. Breathe in trust, as Scrooge did. It is when Scrooge let go of his fear that he began reaching for the light of truth. Allow the light of truth to envelop and strengthen you. Know this with certainty—there is nothing in the past that is too horrendous that we cannot face together with the truth as our guide.

Now, I am sure that even within the words of the first paragraph of this exploration, there will be skeptics. These naysayers of self-improvement and internal renewal will be clouded by their own cynicism. Their cynicism will have them proclaim, "Here we go: yet another touchy-feely book that wants all its readers to have a pity party for themselves. A relationship with our true self—isn't it time to move on?" Moreover, there will be some who scoff at any idea of self-discovery, believing it to be rubbish (humbug). Further still, they will think that this time spent on self-discovery is simply another opportunity for individuals to blame others rather than take responsibility for themselves. Some will believe that this kind of thinking is what leads to self-centeredness, which creates further apathy in a world that is already at the point of no return. I address this pessimism by explaining my fervent belief that when we take the time to examine and unravel our true selves, we become more cognizant of our connectedness to those around us. As a result, we become aware of how our true purpose is meant to enhance the world. More importantly, we realize how momentous our social connectedness is with each individual sharing this universe. This greater mindfulness of our true self evaporates the critical messages of difference despite race, gender, religion, sexual orientation, and ethnic background. We move from apathy to empathy, shifting ourselves from self-centeredness to connectedness.

As you move through this book and the exercises within it, it will return you to the miracle that you are and always have been since your conception. More importantly, the reacquainting of your true self and your spiritual self will bring about an empowerment that will lead you to eagerly move forward in your life, embracing the true call of your purpose. The coalescing of the true self and spiritual self will call you to rise up to your pure purpose and meaning.

The next gift bequeathed to you on this journey is increased understanding and meaning in all your relationships. This book will bring clarity to your relationships on all levels. Specifically, it will show how your abandonment of the gift that is you has led you to participate in cyclical relationships and behaviors that reinforce humbug messages intended to guide you away from true happiness. The journey within this book is meant to reintroduce you to the relationship of the gift you truly are and the happiness that is your birthright.

The Gift

From a cocoon-like sleep,
Life stirred with voices echoing.
Awaken, my child, to the world at hand.
Fear not...
It is I, your parent,
Who will cradle you.
It is I, your parent,
Who will nurture and care for you.
Awaken, my child, to the world at hand.
Want not...
It is I, your parent,
Who will provide.
It is I, your parent,
Who will guide.
Come, my child, from your cocoon
To the world at hand.
Awaken, my child, to the world at hand.
Unfurl the gift that is you, my child,
To the world at hand.
Reveal the beauty that is you, my child,
To the world at hand.
Fear not...
It is I, your parent,
Who will hear your sorrow.
It is I, your parent,
Who will bear your pain.
Awaken, my child, to the word at hand.
It is I, your parent,
Who will remember the miracle on the way.
Awaken, my child.
It is I, your parent,
Who will celebrate the gift given to me this day.

—D. Gibbs

If I Only Had A...

As we continue to journey from humbug to happiness, it is necessary for us to take a detour from our current destination. The detour is brief but crucial from this point forward. It is the foundation that this journey is built upon. It is the cornerstone that sets *Humbug to Happiness* apart from all other journeys of self-discovery. The detour will be much like that of a young girl searching for a wizard in the Land of Oz.

The search will be one that is filled with wonderful opportunities of self-awareness and discovery. However, I must also warn you. Our friend traveling to Oz happened upon characters whose primary mission was to derail her journey to Emerald City. For you, this detour may conjure nefarious and maleficent characters who unwittingly cast the dark spell of the humbug messages over your true purpose and gift.

The dark spells of the humbug messages are much like those of the Wicked Witch of the West, who is filled with her own internal angst.

Having been imprisoned by the internal battles of their own humbug messages eroding their true purposes and gifts over time, these characters inadvertently lash out. Feeling helpless and paralyzed by the heaviness of their eroded sense of self, the pain begins to percolate within them. Having no release, they reach a boiling point. They cackle, sending hideous humbug messages to those within their grasp. The powerful force of the frightening cackle is received and absorbed in the minds of their innocent victims.

Once the humbug message is absorbed, it sets into motion the erosion of the fragile sense of self. This degradation of the mind's landscape engenders the wounded state of being that blinds its victims from truly finding their gift or true purpose.

As we continue to unravel the mystery of our own humbug messages, we must be as courageous as a lion, as sensitive as a tinman, and as brainy as a scarecrow.

If you are willing, we will move on down the brick road together. Together, arm in arm, we will finally reach our destination to our own Emerald City. As we travel on, we will ease down our own brick road that draws us closer to the baffling but brilliant paths we have traveled and the paths yet to be taken.

My friends, the road that lies ahead in this journey points directly to the center of all that we are. It is the journey to our own Emerald City, the magnificent and powerful city that is the brain.

The brain is truly the all-knowing and powerful wizard that we have been searching for. By understanding the brain, we will come to the realization that in the end, we lack nothing. More baffling, we have had the ability to return home to our true purpose at any time during our journey. Our friends in Oz came to realize this at the end of their journey. This realization was proclaimed by the good witch, Glinda—each of our beloved characters already possessed the gifts they searched tirelessly for. The gift of going home was just a couple of shoe clicks away for Dorothy.

The awkward, straw-filled Scarecrow shares with Dorothy his desire to find the wizard in the hopes of being granted a brain. However, as our friends traveled, it was the Scarecrow who had the brains to get them all to Oz.

The Tinman exclaimed to Dorothy, "If I only had a heart!" So Dorothy welcomes the Tinman on her quest in search of the wizard. During their trek to the wizard, it is the Tinman who shows great sensitivity to all his companions. Lastly, the Cowardly Lion believes he could be king of the forest if the wizard just granted him courage. Although outwardly the Lion trembles and quivers with fear, he displays great bravery on their way to see the wizard. Unfortunately, our dear friends are caught in the labyrinth of their sense of lacking, wandering aimlessly and waiting for someone else to provide them direction. More horrifically, Dorothy and her friends unknowingly perpetuate their sense of lacking as they continually reinvest in immobilizing humbug messages. Our friends huddled together, exclaiming, "Lions and tigers and bears—oh my!"

Much like our friends in Oz, many of us search tirelessly for someone or something to provide the answer of our true purpose. For some, the task of uncovering our true purpose or gift becomes too arduous. The laborious task seems futile, so we seek to numb the nagging humbug messages in hopes of escaping them. Blinded by our sense of lacking and feelings of resentment, anger, rejection, and fear, we are held captive. The fear dangles over our lives, much like the flying monkeys who soared above our friends in Oz. The flying monkeys are released with the intention of keeping our friends in a constant state of fear. More insidiously, they fly above as a constant reminder of our friends' investments in their fear-based belief that there is no way home. Further, there is no escaping their own sense of lacking within their core messages: "If I only had a brain, if I only had a heart, if I only had courage," and "if I only had a way home." Much like our friends in Oz, many of us are held captive by our own "monkeys." Sadly, the fear from our own "monkeys" will become so daunting that many people will acquiesce and fade deeper into our addictive states of being.

Once again, they are imprisoned by the humbug messages. They are fettered by the statement, "If I only had a..."

Today, I make a plea to them, as well as to all those who are participating in this journey. I ask that you breathe in *courage* and exhale your doubt and fear. Enveloped by our courage, we will continue our journey, shoulder to shoulder and side by side, moving rhythmically toward the epicenter of all that we are. Linked arm in arm, our destination is seen with complete clarity now. As we continue traveling down the cobblestone path, we edge closer and closer to the city where the wonderful wizard resides.

Finally reaching our destination, we throw back the curtain to reveal the truth that is the all-knowing and all-powerful wizard—the brain. As we stand in complete awe of the splendid design that is the brain, we recognize that it is our journey within the pages of *Humbug to Happiness* that has led us to our destination.

The brain as a tabula rasa, or blank slate, as discussed in the chapter "Thawing the Gift," introduced the idea that at birth, our minds (brains) are blank slates. However, to simply say the brain is a blank slate may appear to minimize the magnificence of this amazing organ. Further, that minimization may cause some to question the validity of the journey we have been on.

In his essay "Concerning Human Understanding in the Seventeenth Century," John Locke says, "the mind is, at birth, a blank slate without rules for processing." This may provide a better springboard for our investigation of the brain. As we dive into the brain, we will uncover exactly what is meant by Locke's statement that our brain is a tabula rasa, or blank slate, without rules for processing.

In understanding the brain as a blank slate, I ask that you contemplate the photograph in figure 5 of a plasma ball. Using the plasma ball as an illustration of our brain, we come to admire the power that lies within.

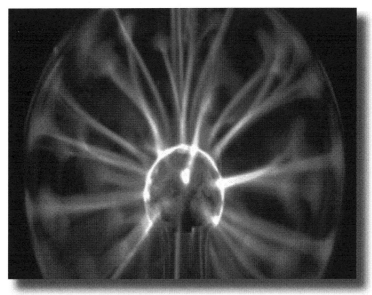

Figure 5. Plasma Ball.

In much of my group and individual therapy, I use the plasma ball as a visual representation of our brain. As we come into this world as an infant, our brain is open and prepared to absorb all the sensory life lessons we will acquire over the span of our early development.

As discussed earlier, technology continues to make advancements in neuroimaging, and the intricate details of the brain have emerged. We now understand that at birth, we are equipped with almost all the neurons (brain cells) we will require. We are prepared with all the neurons that will be required to begin the tasks of imprinting on the tabula rasa (brain).

As we experience the world through our senses, the brain establishes the necessary connections between the sensory experience and the neurons. This relationship, once established, becomes part of our cache of memories. This relationship is essential, in that it allows us to retrieve the messages or experience from our unconscious mind. The cache of memories becomes part of either the conscious or the unconscious. The conscious mind holds information that we are keenly aware of. The unconscious mind holds all the sensory information from all our life experiences—the good, the bad, and the ugly of life. The reality is that as infants and children, we do not have the capacity to prioritize what stays or goes.

In an effort to recognize the simplicity of retrieving a message from the unconscious, I ask that you participate in this brief exercise. Take a deep breath, and relax. Now, I would like for you to remember your favorite holiday or your favorite birthday. Allow your mind to travel back to that time. Allow your mind to recall the sights, the sounds, the people, and the aroma of this time.

I can say with certainty that most of you were able to retrieve that moment in time. The retrieval of that experience is a result of your five senses absorbing all the magical moments of that event. Your brain, triggered by the request, becomes activated.

The neurons fire and travel through the neurological network of memories associated with your holiday or birthday. More importantly, chemicals are released within the neural pathways that have an association to the holidays that were filled with pleasant experiences. Similar to a photograph, these memories are quickly called up as the result of your sensory experience of the particular holiday or birthday. As the result of imprinting, the sensory experience of that holiday or birthday allows you the ability to retrieve, from the cache of memories, a particular moment in time. So astonishing is this process within our brain that some of you may have been able to retrieve a particular smell of what was cooking on the stove that day, the faces of the people there, or the laughter that filled the entire space on that special day.

Another experience I refer to during my session with clients is one from early child development—the lesson of learning to tie a shoe. The lesson of tying our shoes is one that we all share in our early development. How did you learn to tie your shoe?

How many of you remember the bunny rabbit poem?

The bunny rabbit poem is one of the tools that many parents and teachers have used to aid in the teaching of this required developmental skill:

> Bunny ears, bunny ears, playing by a tree.
> Crisscrossed the tree, trying to catch me.
> Bunny ears, bunny ears, jumped into the hole.
> Popped out the other side, beautiful and bold.

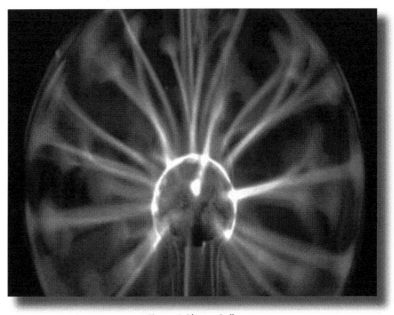

Figure 6. Plasma Ball.

Again, utilizing the plasma ball as our guide in understanding the connection between our senses and our brain, we will break down the process that we all have mastered—the art of tying our shoes.

First, I think we all agree that at birth, we were not equipped with the knowledge or ability to tie our shoes. However, with the proper imprinting (bunny rabbit poem) on the tabula rasa, as well as the art of repetitiveness through practice, a child will successfully tie his or her shoes with ease. Further, as the child becomes better at tying his or her shoes, the magnificent wizard that is the brain will begin to "prune" the unnecessary connections related to this task. Specifically, when we bend down to tie our shoes today, we do it with great ease and very little thought. This efficient process is a result of the natural practice of "pruning."

The brain, a magical wizard, naturally removes (prunes) areas of the neurological network that are no longer needed or unnecessary. Once a skill is achieved through repeated practice, the brain adjusts to complete a task in the most efficient way possible.

In completing the rudimentary journey of the brain, it is necessary to return to the purpose of *Humbug to Happiness* and its connection to the brain.

Consider the following: at birth, we are not equipped to complete the task of tying our shoes, as the brain is a blank slate. More significantly, our brain is simply lacking the necessary data or imprinting to complete the task.

If you agree with this premise, then consider that there must be truth in the message of *Humbug to Happiness*—that each of us, upon our arrival, are pure and innocent gifts of love with unlimited potential. Further, any distortion is a result of life experiences that have been cast upon us unwittingly by those dearest to us. As alluded to earlier, it is not my intention to cast blame on parents, religious affiliations, or society. However, it is my goal to assist you in identifying the humbug messages that have continued to fetter you, holding you captive in the darkness deep within you.

It is my hope that the stories of the amazing men and women who have taken their own journey have assisted you during your journey!

Humbug Scenario III

Early in my career, I had an amazing opportunity to be a fifth-grade teacher. The experience of being a teacher is one that I still speak of with pride and joy. It was here that I first recognized the power of the humbug messages imprinted on the tabula rasa, or blank slate, of developing masterpieces. Specifically, I will share the story of an outstanding young boy, whom I will call M. He was always well groomed and came prepared every day. M worked tirelessly to achieve the highest standard in all his classes. However, on a Friday, during the expected weekly current-events test, M was beginning to unravel. He was sitting in the back of the room and outwardly expressed his frustration, stating, "Mr. Gibbs, are you sure the answers are in here?"

I assured M and the entire class that all the answers to the test could be found in the newspaper. Furthermore, if they had thoroughly read the paper the night before, they should all be successful. Recognizing M's continued struggle, I asked him to come to my desk. I asked what he was struggling with. He said that he had one unanswered question. I asked why he was getting so upset, as he had done quite well up to that point answering the questions.

M said, "Mr. Gibbs, can't you just give me the answer?"

Of course, I told him no—that I couldn't just provide the answer, but if he continued to look in the paper, he could find it. M returned to his desk no less burdened. After a little more time had passed, he began to unravel once more, again requiring me to call him to my desk. However, now M had tears in his eyes. I asked about the frustration that had brought tears to this young boy.

He said, "Mr. Gibbs, I have to get a hundred percent. I have to get an A."

I said, "M, it's just one test." I explained to him that it appeared he had only missed one question on the entire test. It was M's response that I think of on a daily basis. It shows the gravity of the humbug messages, whether they are spoken or unspoken, and the impact they have on the developing masterpieces of the world.

M said, "Mr. Gibbs, anything less than an A is just not good enough. My parents expect more from me."

After hearing his reply, I shared with M that he was more than a grade, that he was an amazing young man with great potential. Receiving a B or even a C on one test didn't change that. I also encouraged M to reach out when he was struggling before he became overwhelmed. Once M asked for help calmly, I sent him back to his desk with more instruction to assist in tracking down the answer. Most importantly, I believe I sent him back to his desk with much more. I sent him back with the understanding that he is more than a grade and more than the perfect child. M was sent back to his desk with an understanding of what his true value was.

Humbug Message Exercise: Love/Belonging Needs

Figure 7. Maslow's Hierarchy of Needs.

In the scenario above, M's humbug message was that he was unworthy if he wasn't perfect. His desire to please his parents engendered a sense of lacking in the areas of acceptance, approval, or love if he did not excel in all his endeavors.

1. How did you get attention?
2. Whose attention did you need but feel it was not received?
3. Were you expected to achieve or behave a certain way?
4. When did you feel most recognized or affirmed?
5. Have you ever had a sense that you just could never measure up to the expectation?
6. When did you feel most unsure that you belonged?

Assignment: Affirmation Fishbowl

Things you will need:

Medium-sized fishbowl, paper, scissors, marker

1. Write a number of positive affirmations on the piece of paper, leaving enough space between the affirmations to cut between them.
2. Take the scissors, and cut the affirmations from the paper.
3. Place affirmation strips in the fishbowl.
4. Each day, pull an affirmation from the fishbowl.
5. Read the affirmation aloud.
6. Place the affirmation where you will have access to it throughout the day.
7. Write out the affirmation at least five times during the day.
8. Read the mantra each time you see the strip.
9. When you go to bed, pin or tape the affirmations on your wall or corkboard so they're visible to you.
10. Repeat until all the affirmations are out of the fishbowl.
11. When the fishbowl is empty, place all affirmations back into the fishbowl, and repeat.

If you put a small value on yourself,
rest assured the world will not raise your price.

—Unknown

The Delivery

n a city far, far away, in the dark night sky, countless stars gleam, as if to say, "This will be a night of glad tidings. This is a moment that will be etched in time." As the universe dances in anticipation, the world welcomes the newborn child. Although the world is in chaos and pain, the child is delivered into waiting and desiring arms. The mother, who carried in her womb the miracle that will be shared with the world, will exalt the child in his glory. The child is a unique and remarkable gift unlike any other—a gift to be cherished, loved, and celebrated. In unison with the mother, the father beams with pride as he looks upon his namesake. Stricken quietly with joy-filled tears, he recognizes that this gift is an extension of the identity that he once had. It is a moment of remembrance, in the midst of the internal pain and sadness of his daily life, of the miracle he once was.

Joyfully, the mother and father had shared the yearning and anticipation of the gift. Hearing the news, everyone beams with joy about this miracle birth. All are enamored, even if for a short time, by the purity of the unconditional love that this birth will bestow to all in its presence.

The ancestors foretold the child's birth into the world. The announcement of the child's arrival leads to exuberant celebration and preparation. While still in the womb, this gift stirs the hearts and memories of those whose life, even if for a brief time, intersect with the gift. Those fortunate enough to experience this reverberate with a mystical stir, which rattles the depths of the layered bitterness from a life unfulfilled. So, in awe of the life in their presence, they yield. This provides many moments of reflection, opportunities to offer a blessing to the mother who carries the gift in her womb, and a chance to visit the cache of memories of their journeys into this world. The cache floods the chasms of their memories. They know the gifts they once were. Like a surging river cascading beyond the banks, the memories flood in—of hope, joy, and the gift of an etched purpose on the day of birth. They are baptized with renewal, rebirth, and a stirring of the spirit. Sadly, most will begin to fear this freedom and return to the hoax of the humbug messages, which close the gates of change. The flood is prevented from reminding them of their gifts of potential and worthiness. The humbug messages demand they return to their habitual and familiar ways of thinking.

Their thoughts are riddled with messages of deception and trickery. They ruminate in doubt and uncertainty. Finally, the spirit of hope in the miracle they once were begins to fade again, into the dark and deep chasm of their sense of lacking. The flickering flame of hope is put out, the vision of the gift darkened once again.

They return to the gift of the new child. As they contemplate the journey of the new arrival, they repress their thoughts about the harsh world that lies ahead for him or her, thoughts that would slowly erode the true gift of a child. The thoughts are of the often harsh reality of the hustle and bustle of a world in chaos. For some, the story of this chapter will resonate with a message of a birth written about by scribes thousands of years ago, a birth that was the foundation of a foreshadowing of a man's character that would leave an indelible mark on the world as we know it—a man, just a man, who, through his words and actions, provided the most significant understanding of human dignity and respect. But the story within this chapter is not about the man but the significance of the birth of a child, the birth of a child we have great knowledge of, the delivery of a child who will be like no other, the delivery of a uniquely designed gift that will leave its distinctive imprint on the world. Who is the child I speak of?

The child I speak of is the miracle that is the child within you. Sadly, the point of this chapter is to bring awareness to the forgotten truth of our birth—the simple truth that our coming into this world was a significant occurrence in time. So what has altered our awareness of our magnificent and miraculous arrival? More noteworthy, what is it that has adulterated and blurred our vision of the miracle of our birth?

The answer, I am afraid, will be one that we must all take some culpability in. Our delivery into this world is now dictated by the timelines of a deductible and copay, a beast that hurries the process of our delivery to the point of becoming a conveyor belt of flesh—the beast of time, the beast of money, the beast of greed, the beast of staying busy enough not to notice I am losing the very thing that is most valuable. The gift of life.

In our self-induced misery, we remember that there will be planes to catch and bills to pay. It is a world so enamored with technology that cruel and demeaning words will be delivered with fierce and grievous intention, where perception rules and truth is lacking. It is a world where billions exist, but fear of differences creates isolation, a world filled with individuals who have forgotten the miracle that exists within. It is a world where falling for anything leaves fewer standing for something, a perfectly imperfect world. It is a world that has been given a gift of a child who is a pure source of love. This child is delivered as a gift to bring hope to the hopeless and a sense of awe to a world dulled by oversaturation. This is a child who embodies vulnerability in a world that perpetuates the need of being on guard—the child we once were but have long since forgotten, having become captivated more by the collection of things and less of the miracles of the human spirit.

Freedom Within

In a moment, the music will begin, and he will again
Touch the freedom that comes from within.

There, in those moments, he can completely be
Open,
Uncensored,
And spiritually free.

Pushing his body, demanding the best,
He puts his dreams and abilities to the test.

It wasn't always easy—
Freedom for him has grown.
But he has taken the emotions of dance
And entwined them with his own.

Never seeking anyone's acceptance,
He found it in some friends
Who watch in awe, respect, and love,
Until the moment ends.

But the moment never really ends;
This freedom keeps on growing.

Those lucky enough to share are grateful to him
For showing that buried dreams,
Once condemned to darkened chambers therein,
Can manifest themselves into
Glorious freedoms within.

—P. Wilson

We must develop and maintain the capacity to forgive. He who is devoid of the power to forgive is devoid of the power to love. There is some good in the worst of us and some evil in the best of us. When we discover this, we are less prone to hate our enemies.

—Martin Luther King Jr.

Le Jour Est Arrivé (The Day Has Come)

A s we inch closer and closer to the end of our journey, I believe it is this chapter that will have the most significant impact. It is here that your willingness to be completely transparent with yourself regarding your true motives will come to the surface. The suggestions encouraged within this chapter will bring you face to face with your truth. In this moment of truth, what will be asked of you may be so unfathomable that you may choose to throw the book down as an abomination, believing it to be yet another self-help book that had no benefit whatsoever. Or you may find it to be an amazing manuscript that has offered an epiphany that will provide a cathartic shift from this moment forward that will allow you to experience life in a new and electrifying way.

However, for you to achieve the latter, you will have to take one of the most significant steps in your path to healing and emotional recovery, an action that is of utmost importance. This action has been written and spoken of for centuries. One man in history made such an impact that his actions remain as the most poignant acts written about in history. At the pinnacle of this man's life, he experienced the most horrific degradation by those he most trusted, according to the scribes of the past. Those he called his followers degraded him. This man was Jesus.

During one of the most heinous acts in history, while suffering beyond comprehension, Jesus lifted his head to the sky and said, "Father, forgive them, for they know not what they are doing." Jesus spent no time wallowing in resentment. He spoke no words of retaliation or revenge, nor did he seek out vengeance. He spoke only of forgiveness for those who had disowned him.

It is my belief that no matter what your faith, it is the story *behind* the story of the crucifixion of Jesus that we are meant to grapple with and understand. It is in understanding the action of the man, as well as the definition of crucifixion, that will draw us closer to the purpose of *Humbug to Happiness*.

The definition that I most want us to consider is that which defines crucifixion as an extremely difficult trials or torturous suffering.

Returning to the story of Jesus, when he was at his most vulnerable state, he spoke words of forgiveness for those who had spent time spitting on him and belittling him. These men and women spent time mocking and minimizing the gifts Jesus offered, gifts given to the duplicitous characters, who at one time or another had been in their own states of suffering.

We must understand the significance of the benevolent act of asking forgiveness. Many of us sit in a cesspool of resentment, harboring the injustice or extreme suffering inflicted by those who have done us wrong either by word or deed. These resentments keep us tightly attached to the experience, whether the injustice was yesterday or decades ago. The word *resentment* is defined as "a feeling of indignant displeasure or persistent ill will at someone or something regarded as a wrong, insult, or injury." So when we make a conscious choice to hold on to resentments, we make a choice to sit in displeasure or persistent ill will. We then become addicted to the emotional states attached to this paralyzing decision. Certainly, I trust that by now in our journey, you have been equipped with the skills to comprehend the gravity of such a decision. This is a decision, consciously made, that continues to shackle us to our misery. We forge this chain, link by link and yard by yard.

I predict with some certainty that a number of people are experiencing indignation toward me. I would like to address these individuals now. Please trust me when I say that I understand the pain, the hurt, and the sadness that burdens you from the injustice done to you. You did not deserve the injustice or wrongdoing—nobody does. The injustice or wrongdoing may have been in the form of physical abuse, sexual abuse, or emotional abuse. It may have been a mother or father abandoning you or you feeling not good enough. You did not deserve to have the gift that is you minimized or devalued in any way. However, I beg you to consider this message. When you hold on to your resentment, you are reliving the injustice or wrongdoing over and over and over again. You then end up with the same outcome.

My friend, if nothing changes, nothing changes. The message of the crucifixion story is that to truly set your spirit free, you must be willing to release all resentment and allow forgiveness. The forgiveness is not about those who have hurt you. It is to free yourself from the internal destruction that prevents you from living your true purpose fully.

It has been in my work as a trained therapist in eye-movement desensitization and reprocessing (EMDR) that the releasing of resentment and offering forgiveness is most significant. I assist the client in returning to a point in his or her life when the feeling of resentment took root. Upon discovering the origins of the resentment, the client and I work at reprocessing the memory to bring about a release of the resentment, opening a potential doorway to forgiveness. Those individuals who have been open and willing to practice this action of forgiveness have reported feeling lighter and much more at peace.

The Dalai Lama addressed the concept of forgiveness in Sydney, Australia, in 2013. The Dalai Lama spoke of five simple life strategies. (Australia 2013) One of the strategies of a simple life is the need to practice forgiveness. He expounded further on the action of forgiveness by saying that the act of forgiveness does not mean accepting the other person's wrongdoing; rather, it is an action that benefits the mental and physical well-being of the one granting the forgiveness.

In closing this chapter, I leave you with the Serenity Prayer. Although adopted by Alcoholics Anonymous and many twelve-step programs, it is attributed to the theologian and ethician Reinhold Niebuhr.

> Give me grace to accept with serenity
> The things that cannot be changed,
> Courage to change the things
> which should be changed,
> And the wisdom to distinguish
> The one from the other.

This prayer is a powerful reminder that in the end, we are the sole landlord of the house within. As we examine the prayer, we need to be reminded of the following things.

The things that cannot be changed:

We *cannot* change the past—how someone has treated us, how someone neglected us, or how someone has hurt us.

The *courage* to change the things that should be changed:

We *can* change our thoughts about the past, our feelings/emotions about the past, and, finally, *our reactions*.

Le Jour Est Arrivé (The Day Has Arrived)

> The day has arrived for acceptance.
> The day has arrived for compassion.
> The day has arrived for understanding.
> The day has arrived for peace.
> The day has arrived for love.
> The day has arrived for forgiveness.
> The time is now…
> —D. Gibbs

Humbug Message Exercise: Forgiveness of Self

Martin Luther King Jr. suggested we must maintain the capacity to forgive. It is my assertion that if we do not have the capacity to first forgive ourselves, we will lack the willingness to forgive others.

In this exercise, take time to rewrite or create your own forgiveness letter. Once you have completed the forgiveness letter, read the letter to yourself at least two times each day: in the morning as you start your day and again at bedtime.

Today I release myself from the shackles of the shame and guilt of my past. Today I forgive myself. As I forgive myself, I recognize that I am human, and as such, I am made of flesh and bone. I recognize that, being part of the human race, I am fallible. I am not identified by my mistakes. I move beyond them and forgive myself today.

Today I release the sense of being a failure or being insignificant. Today I forgive myself for the hurt I may have caused others by either my words or my actions. Today I release my internal sense of shame for neglecting those who needed my love and support. Today I realize that I am forgiven. Today I recognize that I am somebody. Today I recognize that I am deserving of all good things.

In understanding forgiveness, I release the resentments I have toward others so that I can live fully in the miracle of my true purpose. Today I rise like a phoenix from the ashes of my past. I will spread my wings of peace and forgiveness as gratitude carries me to the unlimited future that is ahead of me. Today I am forgiven. Today I am capable of forgiveness. Forgiveness fills every cell of my body. I breathe in forgiveness each and every day.

Humbug Message Exercise: Thoughts on Forgiving Others

When you hold resentment toward another, you are bound to that person or condition by an emotional link that is stronger than steel. Forgiveness is the only way to dissolve that link and get free.

—Catherine Ponder

To forgive is the highest, most beautiful form of love. In return, you will receive untold peace and happiness.

—Robert Muller

The weak can never forgive. Forgiveness is the attribute of the strong.

—Mahatma Gandhi

True forgiveness is when you are able to say, "Thank you for that experience."

—Oprah Winfrey

Climbing the Waterspout

The best thing about the future is that it comes one day at a time.

—Abraham Lincoln

One day at a time—this is enough. Do not look back and grieve over the past, for it is gone; and do not be troubled about the future, for it has not yet come. Live in the present, and make it so beautiful that it will be worth remembering.

—Ida Scott Taylor

The Bible speaks of new beginnings and tells us to "forget the past and look forward to what lies ahead."

—Philippians 3:13–14 (New King James Bible)

As I contemplate the task of finding the most fitting conclusion to our journey from humbug to happiness, I am filled with both excitement and trepidation. The excitement is in knowing that you have successfully come to the end of your journey. This fills me with hope for you and the new path of happiness you have embarked upon. The trepidation stems from my own humbug messages of "Was it good enough?" and "Will they look forward to their new beginnings?"

In truth, the excitement of writing about a new beginning caused my vision to blur. Then I recognized that my perfectionism was getting in the way. More importantly, the answer to what I needed to say in closing was right under my nose. I realized that the possibilities of a new beginning inundate us in various forms throughout each and every day of our lives.

First and omnipresent for all of us is today—the *present*. It is a new beginning, something we are all blessed with each and every sunrise. I am made personally aware of this daily, as I am awakened in the morning by the sounds of birds chirping outside my window. I open my eyes and breathe in the possibilities of this new day. As I exhale, I speak a message of gratitude to the universe for the gift of this day. I celebrate the new beginning that I have been given on this day. The struggles of yesterday are laid to rest. I know I have completed the work to maintain healthy living. Further, nothing should burden me any longer, as all of yesterday has retired with the sunset. So it is a perfectly designed gift that each day is a starting point, a beginning, and the origin of something new. So jump for joy in the present!

The second and most obvious experience that trumpets a new beginning is the glorious day of your awakening into this world. It was at the moment of your first breath that the universe celebrated your gift. More significantly, the universe yearns to move in unison with your true purpose. Working in harmony with your true purpose, the universe is aware of your pure energy source. This perfect alignment of the rhythm of the universe and your pure energy source is designed so that in the sharing of your gift, you can achieve unlimited success. The announcement of your birth rang in beautiful harmony with the magnificent orchestra of the universe. Our birthdays, those unique and special days each year, are when we reflect on the day our amazing journeys began, the starting points of our design.

However, the intention of this yearly ritual is not to simply recognize our chronological ascent that draws us closer to the dreaded marker of over the hill. We are all called to regenerate, to extinguish the old to make way for a rebirth or a new beginning each and every day. As you move through this journey, you are challenged to experience a rebirth. This rebirth is meant to restore you to a better, higher, and more worthy state. This is the birth that the universe or your higher power had intended as yours by design. Everyone deserves a life filled with joy. There is happiness enough for everyone. No individual who has been brought into this world should fear that there is not enough. There is enough for everyone to experience an abundance of peace, love, acceptance, and worthiness to the end of his or her days. As we draw near to the end of this journey together, take a deep breath. Say to yourself at this very moment, "Happy birthday! The universe danced the day I was born!"

In our early development, we are provided many messages of a new beginning in forms that may appear, at first, to be benign. However, if one delves a little deeper, a simple nursery rhyme attempts to relay a message that a new beginning is always an option. More importantly, a new beginning is a possibility—no matter how many obstacles get in our way.

"Itsy Bitsy Spider" (also known as "Incy Wincy Spider" and several other similar-sounding names) is a popular nursery rhyme that describes the adventures of a spider as it ascends, descends, and then ascends again the downspout of a gutter system.

Let's have some fun. Go ahead, read the nursery rhyme. Really take the time to read the rhyme.

> The itsy-bitsy spider
> Climbed up the waterspout.
> Down came the rain
> And washed the spider out.

Out came the sun
And dried up all the rain.
And the itsy-bitsy spider
Climbed up the spout again.

I am going to take a guess right now. In reading the nursery rhyme, there are many of you who couldn't get through this nursery rhyme without singing the phrases. I can also predict that a great number of you remembered the hand movements that accompanied the singing of this rhyme. Even more exciting, some of you started to laugh or giggle during your attempt to remember the particular hand movements. How is it that I can predict the behavior of some of you? The answer to this question has been woven throughout the previous pages of *Humbug to Happiness*.

As discussed earlier, we have stored memories that rest in the unconscious—what we will call a cache. This consists of a multitude of stored files that hold memories from early in our development. These memories become imprinted in the neural pathways of our brains. These memories include the good, the bad, and the ugly of our life experiences to that point. Those memory files can be triggered at any moment and time. Once triggered, the neural pathways of our brains with attachments to the experiences begin to fire. We are taken in our minds to the time and place that lesson was learned. So you and I will sing the nursery rhyme while remembering the hand movements that accompany it. This occurs as a result of the memories that were imprinted early in our innocent school days, during our introduction to this industrious and persistent arachnid.

So, let's get back to that spider! Of course, we can all predict what the spider has been doing since we last left it. The spider, most certainly, climbed the spout again. Despite the fact that the rain continues to wash the spider out and the rain continues to be an obstacle to this industrious arachnid's desire to reach the top, the spider remains filled with determination. The spider, consistently believing in the unseen, thinks the sun will surely come out. He embraces the opportunity of a new beginning. So, filled with the determination to reach the top of that spout, the spider begins his ascent again and again. This amazingly humorous nursery rhyme is meant to introduce us early in life to an industrious creature with an important life message. Despite having a clear vision of our goals and the journeys we must take to achieve them, life is filled with obstacles. How we face those obstacles will determine the depth of our character. More importantly, those obstacles carve into our faith. Just like the spider, we must have unwavering faith in believing that the sun will surely come out again, no matter how bleak it may appear.

This simple but magnificent story is a reminder that a new beginning is within our grasp when we choose to pick ourselves up rather than stay beaten down by the defeating humbug messages of the past. It is your willingness to persevere that will empower you to make the decision to start the climb once again. This inclination to reach your fullest potential will truly start the transformation to being your own champion in your reclamation.

Once you rise up in recognition of the champion you were meant to be, all things will align in the knowing of your true purpose.

Last, the message of a new beginning becomes the focal point for millions of individuals across the country once a year. It is an attempt to release the past in order to ignite the future. The year ends on December 31, and a new year begins. Many wait with great anticipation as the clock ticks down. This ritual is ripe with the message of an opportunity to start again. Invigorated by this opportunity, millions will gather around friends and family to verbalize their yearning for a new beginning. They proclaim New Year's resolutions to all who will hear. However, some are simply caught up in the fervor of the palpable willingness of others to invest in the ritual, too. This means that their commitments to new beginnings fade slowly into failure once again. Their good intentions become "should have, could have," and "maybe next year."

As discussed earlier, it is your commitment to being open to these suggestions that will bring about change. You, in your unique design, are the key that will unlock the door to your renewal. This renewal is filled with opportunity for a new perspective on your life.

With the new awareness that we are sensory beings, you recognize that this journey has been absorbed at some level. With that understanding comes great responsibility. I must provide a cautionary word.

It will become increasingly more uncomfortable for you to embrace the old patterns of thought that led to the cycle of your unhealthy behavior. No matter how hard you may try to block this message of change, your brain has already absorbed that you are a miracle. Your brain will begin to fire within the newly developed neurological pathways of change. Once the imprinting and firing have been established, from that moment on, there will be unease when you are tempted to fall back into your old patterns of thinking—patterns that eventually lead you to old behaviors.

Nothing changes if nothing changes, and if I keep doing what I've always done, I'll keep getting what I've always got and will keep feeling what I always felt.

—Unknown

Humbug Message Exercise: Be the Spider

In the nursery rhyme "Itsy Bitsy Spider," we discover just how determined that spider was to reach its goal to climb the waterspout. In this exercise, take time to list your goals. Goals are defined as the object of a person's ambition or effort, an aim, or desired result. Goals can be short term or long term. Ask yourself, what are my goals for today? What are my short- and long-term goals? To assist you in understanding goals, use this helpful acronym:

Grounded—Be realistic in setting goals for yourself.

Observable—When assessing your progress toward your goals, you should be able to identify the specific things you accomplished to attain your goals.

Action—To attain your goals, it will require action each and every day.

Laid out—Take time to write out your goals. Create a clear and detailed guide that you can refer to everyday as a reminder. Additionally, review it any time that you may feel you have strayed from the path toward your goals.

Specific—Be very specific about what your goals are. Leave no doubt in your mind or in others' minds exactly what goals you want to achieve.

My goals today are:

My short-term goals are:

My long-term goals include:

Your Life Holds Unlimited Potential and Wonderful Dreams

You have the ability
to attain whatever you seek.
Within you is every potential
you can imagine.

Always aim higher than
you believe you can reach.
So often, you'll discover
that when your talents are set free
by your imagination,
you can achieve any goal.

If people offer their
help or wisdom
as you go through life,
accept it gratefully.
You can learn much from those
who have gone before you.

But never be afraid or hesitant
to step off the accepted path
and head off in your own direction
if your heart tells you
that it's the right way for you.

Always believe that you will
ultimately succeed
at whatever you do
and never forget the value
of persistence, discipline,
and determination.
You are meant to be
whatever you dream of becoming.

—Edmund O'Neill

No Place like Home

S o, my friends, in closing, I leave you exactly where we began—a place you are most familiar with. The place called *home*.

Home is knowing. Knowing your mind, knowing your heart, knowing your courage.

—The Wizard of Oz

You have always had the power...[You] just had to learn it for [your]self.

—The Wizard of Oz

Furthermore, I leave you with this. To embrace a total transformation leading to your new beginning, it will require from you an investment in a decision that has no alternatives. You and I already have the knowledge of the outcomes when we have invested in the compromises within the humbug messages. These compromises are made in an effort to avoid recognizing the one decision you and I must make. Simply put, you can decide today by asking yourself the following questions: Do I choose a total transformation and a new beginning? Or do I choose to remain in the bondage and the prison that are the humbug messages of my past, which have paralyzed my gifts—a bondage that has kept me from achieving the life I have dreamed about?

Now visualize the shackles that have held you captive falling to the ground. As you release yourself from the shackles of the past, breathe in...

> I choose freedom,
> A new beginning,
> Today.
> I choose peace over pain.

The positive thinker sees the invisible, feels the intangible, and achieves the impossible!

—Winston Churchill

Humbug Message Exercise: Daily Self-Assessment

Part of your continuing self-care in moving from humbug to happiness is remembering the conditions that can lead you back to your humbug messages. Each day take a personal inventory to assess whether you are moving toward happiness or returning to your humbug patterns of thought. Use the list below to assist you:

Hungry Oftentimes when we are on the path of change, our habituated patterns of the past will begin to stir. Familiar patterns of your past will have a strong desire or craving to keep you invested in your past humbug patterns of thought. Be aware on a daily basis of assessing your thinking patterns, patterns of thought that stir a strong desire or craving to feel full. Behaviors to consider: attention seeking, approval hunting, eating, drinking, drugging, and relationship searching. These are all external sources that fool you into believing that you are full. Remember to be on top of addressing your hierarchy of needs on a daily basis.

Unsocial Oftentimes when we begin to make significant changes in our life, there is an unrealistic fear of how others will perceive us. Always remember our need for healthy human connection is vital for our mental and spiritual well-being. Remember, isolating leads us oftentimes to participate in our self-defeating thoughts. So connect with supportive friends and family members.

Minimized When we have a sense that we or others are beginning to underestimate our true value, we begin to feel unworthy or undeserving. Feeling unworthy leads to resentment; resentment leads us to slipping back to our old habituated actions connected to our humbug messages of our past. So pick another affirmation out of your affirmation fishbowl.

Bored When we have a sense of boredom, we begin to feel restless and dissatisfied. Oftentimes these feelings of boredom lead us to seek some relief—relief from our old humbug messages that will continue to decay the progress that has been made. To relieve yourself of feeling bored, get up and go for a walk or talk to a supportive friend.

Unworthy When individuals begin to make changes in their lives that shift them from their humbug habituated patterns of thought, they will oftentimes experience a nagging sense that they are undeserving. Know that you must face these thoughts head on. Be sure to be prepared with your list of affirmations that support that you are deserving and worthy of all the good things life has to offer.

Grief Grief is a normal and natural emotional reaction to loss or change of any kind. In itself, grief is neither a pathological condition nor a personality disorder. When making significant change, there is often a sense of loss. If you should experience grief as a result of the sense of loss of your old humbug patterns of thought, begin to make a list of what you have gained or will gain from letting go of the past.

Suggestions to help you when you are experiencing the signs of HUMBUG:

- Early identification is essential.
- Reexamine the stairs of change.
- Call a supportive friend.
- Go for a walk or do some exercise.
- Listen to calming music.
- Participate in something you enjoy—yoga, dance, hiking, singing, a movie, biking, rollerblading, basketball, volleyball, or bowling.
- REMEMBER: This will pass—it is only temporary.

Humbug Message Exercise: the Master Equation Exercise

Through structure and routine, we bring about the greatest changes in our lives. The goal of this exercise is to assist you in creating a daily structure or plan each day. The *master equation* will provide an answer on a daily basis on whether you are moving toward happiness or falling back to your familiar humbug patterns of thinking.

The Master Equation

Monitoring thinking patterns + emotional monitoring (feelings) + physical activity + working on spiritual or universal connectedness = SUCCESS

On a daily basis, follow this guide to assist you in creating a *daily master equation* to keep you on track.

Today I will work on this area of my thinking: _____

Today I will be aware when I am feeling:

_____

If I feel this, I will immediately do the following:

_____

Today I will care for my physical vessel by:

_____

Today I will work on my understanding that I am connected to a greater source of energy by:

_____

When you retire in the evening, take time to assess how well you did. If you had some slips, tell yourself it is okay; it doesn't mean you failed. You are getting better and better at this new way of thinking.

I leave you with a set of questions that I ask myself when I am struggling in any of these areas. These are questions that I use to get myself back on track:

> Is my current thinking right now helping or hurting me?
> Is what I am about to do for my physical vessel helping me achieve my goals?
> Is what I am doing right now going to help me achieve what I want to achieve?
> Is what I am about to do or say adding positively to the greater source energy?

Humbug Message Exercise: A List of Affirmations

The universe provides all that I need to be successful.
I am a magnet that draws positive experiences to my life.
I am deserving of all good things.
People in my life are eager to help me achieve my goals.
I am surrounded by joy and happiness in my life.
The universe is eager to provide me the opportunities that bring success in my life.
I am filled with the energy required to accomplish the tasks in my life.
I have clear and direct ideas to achieve my goals.

My mind is open to the creative process that flows to me.
Healthy relationships surround me.
People are attracted to me.
I am filled with healing and growth.
Money comes to me free and easily.
I am grateful for the wealth in my life.
I feel full and satisfied.
My mind is filled with empowering and helpful thoughts.
I am a uniquely designed source energy that celebrates connectedness with others.
I am a source of love, joy, and peace in the world I am in.

Happiness is mine from this moment forward.
I celebrate the renewal of the miracle that is me today.

BIBLIOGRAPHY

Alcoholics Anonymous World Services, Inc.. New York, New York: 2001. 4th Edition. Print

B. Zoe. 5 Life Lessons from the Dalai Lama: Live 2013 Sydney Event: Simple Life Strategies. 18 June 2013. Web. 12 Dec. 2014

Burtt, Edwin A. The English Philosophers from Bacon to Mill. New York New York: Random, House Inc. 1939 Print

Bryne, Rhonda. The Secret. New York, New York: Artia Books 2006

Corey, Gerald. Theory and Practice of Counseling and Psychotherpy. Pacific Grove, CA: Brooks/Cole Publishing. 1991 4th Edition Print

Hicks, R.D. De Anima. Translated R.D. Hicks. Buffalo, New York: Prometheus Books. 1991. Print

Hoffman, Edward The Right to be Human A Biography of Abraham Maslow. Los Angles, CA.: St. Martins Press. 1988 Print

Maslow, A.H. A Theory of Human Motivation. New York: First Start Publishing 2012. Print

David L. Strayer, Jason M. Watson, and Frank A. Drews, Cognitive Distraction While Multitasking in the Automobile. In Brian Ross, editor: The Psychology of Learning and Motivation, Vol. 54, Burlington: Academic Press, 2011, pp. 29-58.

"Serenity Prayer". Wikipedia. The Free Encyclopedia. The Wikimedia Foundation, Inc., 16 February 2016. Web. 16 February 2016 https://en.wikipedia.org/wiki/Serenity_Prayer

About the Author:

D avid A. Gibbs, PhD, LMHC, CAP, ICADC, is a licensed clinical counselor and certified addiction professional in Florida and Ohio who has more than twenty years of experience counseling in the fields of mental health and substance abuse.

Gibbs has worked in multiple settings, including home-based crisis stabilization, private and nonprofit organizations, and private practice. He presents at both local and national conferences addressing mental health and substance abuse, and their impact on communities.

Made in the USA
Columbia, SC
05 September 2020